Dance Notation for Beginners

√63
√05

LPC

befc

WD

Dance Notation for Beginners

Labanotation
by Ann Kipling Brown FIKL

Benesh Movement Notation
by Monica Parker FIChor

Dance Books Ltd
Cecil Court · London

First published in 1984 by Dance Books Ltd,
15 Cecil Court, London WC2N 4EZ

ISBN 0 903102 71 4

Designed by Ron Jones

Design and production in association with Book Production
Consultants, 47 Norfolk Street, Cambridge.

Typeset by Goodfellow & Egan Ltd, Cambridge

Printed by Hartnolls Limited,
Victoria Square, Bodmin, Cornwall

Contents

Preface

From 1983, the Schools Examinations Board of the University of London has offered a General Certificate of Education Ordinary level examination in Dance. A compulsory component of this examination syllabus is an elementary study of *either* the Benesh *or* the Laban system of dance notation.

This book is designed to meet this requirement. It describes the basic structures of each system and introduces ways in which notation may be used in the analysis and creation of dances.

The practical part of the Examination includes both the performance of a set technical study and the presentation of an original composition in either Classical or Contemporary style. Candidates are *not* expected to read the dance scores of the technical studies nor to notate their compositions. The purpose of the Notation study is "to increase awareness of the language of dance".

Dance Notation provides a systematic means of identifying and investigating movement. Use this introductory book as *part* of your study of dance. The selected movement material is fundamental to many dance styles and techniques. The material is presented without reference to a particular terminology. Elements of movement such as direction, shape and rhythm are as integral to folk dancing as to jazz dancing. Interpret and explore these elements using the dance techniques which you have chosen.

Further material and information may be obtained from,

for Benesh Movement Notation
>> The Benesh Institute
>> 12 Lisson Grove
>> London NW1 6TS

for Labanotation
>> The Language of Dance Centre
>> 17 Holland Park
>> London W11 3TD

Ann Kipling Brown
Monica Parker

Foreword

by Peter Brinson

Principal Lecturer in the Sociology of Dance and Head of the Department of Research and Community Development, Laban Centre for Movement and Dance.

This is one of the most exciting dance books of recent years. For the first time it brings together in one volume the basic structures of two of the most significant systems of dance notation in the world today, certainly the two systems in widest use. Therefore the book represents also an important historical moment in the development of dance and movement notation studies. It opens the way to a huge exploration of mostly untapped human knowledge and experience.

For more than five centuries dance teachers, choreographers and dance thinkers in Europe have tried to devise systems of recording on paper dance steps, gestures and patterns. This has required a search for symbols which could represent the non-verbal language of dance. During my travels round the European archives of ballet in the early 1960s, collecting material for *Background to European Ballet*, I came across records of this search. There were word-abbreviations and letter-symbols in notebooks of the mid-fifteenth century. Arbeau's famous *Orchesographie* of 1588 is testimony to the value of accurate verbal description just as Gautier's vivid evocation of romantic ballet three centuries later illustrates the power of verbal imagery in recapturing a dance performance. Between these events the ballet master Pierre Beauchamp and the dancer/choreographer Raoul Feuillet devised a system which served the dances and ballets of eighteenth century Europe until the technical explorations and expressive demands of romantic, then classical, ballet required a system which could indicate the use of body and arms as well as feet. Hence the symbolic systems of Saint-Léon in France, Zorn in Germany and Stepanoff in Russia during the last half of the nineteenth century.

Our own century has seen not only a great extension of dance art but a more scientific approach to the study of all aspects of human movement. The different symbol systems devised by Rudolf Laban and by Rudolf and Joan Benesh are responses to this wider inquiry into human movement. They are the first really comprehensive notation systems. These systems, however, are the fruit of *European* dance development. What about the rest of the world? Newly discovered America, of course, has adopted European systems, but is it not possible that the ancient dance cultures of India, South-East Asia, China, Japan and elsewhere also have devised dance notation systems now shut away, perhaps, in archives? The history of the world's movement notation has yet to be written just as the use of notation itself is only beginning. Through the development of this notation I am convinced we may see an extension of human knowledge at present very difficult to grasp. "Dance is part of the history of human movement", I wrote in the opening words of the Gulbenkian Foundation's *Dance Education and Training in Britain*, "part of the history of human culture and part of the history of human communication". If it is all these things (and remember that human movement is the source of life, of economic production and civilisation) dance represents a vast area of knowledge and experience, non-verbally acquired and communicated, which we have never before had the means properly to explore. Now, through movement notation and its complementary devices of film and video, we have this possibility.

Not only have the two systems here described already proved themselves in practice; not only is this book a step in their development because it is the first joint publication: the book marks also the first time dance notation has been included in the state school examination system. Thus it opens the way for a far more profound study of dance and movement as a regular part of education than has been possible before. Young people will be able not only to practice dance for themselves but learn from the experience of others, including great masters, through choreographic scores of the past and present. What is possible in dance will be possible also over the whole vast range of human movement, nation by nation, drawing on the knowledge stored within it. London University's G.C.E. 'O' level in dance, supported by this book, is the beginning of much greater things to come.

Labanotation

Acknowledgements

I am particularly indebted to the following people:

Members of the G.C.E. 'O' Level Committee led by Joan White for their encouragement and support in the writing of this textbook.

Friends and colleagues on the staff of the Language of Dance Centre for their time and help in reading, checking and advising on material, in particular to Ann Hutchinson Guest whose work and knowledge has been an inspiration.

The Ballet Rambert and to Jaap Flier, the choreographer, for their permission to use the notated extract.

Claire Teverson for the notation of the extract from the ballet 'Echoi II'.

Abbreviations

R   Right
L   Left
F   Forward
B   Backward
D   Diagonal
P   Practice in Reading and Writing

Introduction

This notation system was originated by Rudolf von Laban (1879–1958) and was first published in his book 'Dance Script' in 1928. Laban's initial interest was dance and he is renowned for his large scale group compositions and work in the theatre. Even though he had considerable influence over contemporary dance forms and a great interest and enthusiasm for the dance he became very involved with the study of movement in its widest sense. He expanded his theories in other spheres and applied his technique of movement analysis to industry, education and recreation. He was specially concerned that his system of notation should serve all areas of human movement. Various people and their respective Centres have helped in the development of the system, notably Albrecht Knust and Ann Hutchinson Guest, so that the notation system can be applied and used by all in the different fields of movement.

This section of the book outlines the basic principles of the Laban system of notation and shows its use in the analysis and composition of dance. It is divided into parts, each part being organised so that the movement idea and the notation can be explored together. In the earlier parts the notation records the general idea behind the movement and allows for exploration and improvisation of a basic movement idea or theme – this is called 'Motif Description' and deals with broad and general statements about movement. Later, these broad statements are gradually defined and greater detail about the movement notated so that a specific and precise description is produced – this is 'Structured Description' in which the exact use of body, time, direction and dynamics is recorded. At the end of each part there is a series of Reading and Writing Exercises to dance which may stimulate ideas for dances of your own, check your understanding of the notated material and assist you in notating your studies and dances. An extract from Jaap Flier's ballet 'Echoi II' has been included for your interest and to show how more and more detail is added to the general movement ideas to produce a precise and exact record.

Further reading materials at different levels to supplement your study may be obtained from the Language of Dance Centre, 17 Holland Park London W11 3TD.

Part 1
Travelling

In travelling the whole body moves *through* space and *across* space – for instance, you can walk, run, jump; or you can perform combinations of these basic activities such as skip, gallop, polka.

Floor Pattern
These travelling activities are performed on a pathway as you travel through and across space. The pathway can either be straight or curved. The arrival point may be the same but the journey can be different.

General Pathways

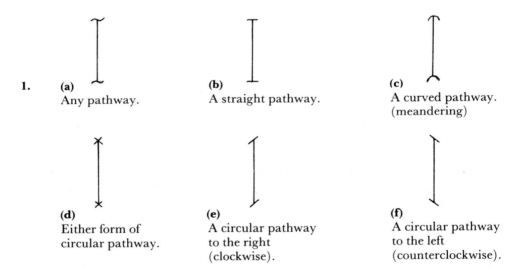

1. (a) Any pathway.

    (b) A straight pathway.

    (c) A curved pathway. (meandering)

    (d) Either form of circular pathway.

    (e) A circular pathway to the right (clockwise).

    (f) A circular pathway to the left (counterclockwise).

For the moment the way in which we travel on a particular pathway will be written in words.

Example: RUN   = Run on a straight pathway.

2.

The Staff

The symbols denoting movement of the whole body are written within a staff. The score is read from the bottom of the page upwards. It always starts with a double bar line and a double bar line at the end indicates that the dance is finished.

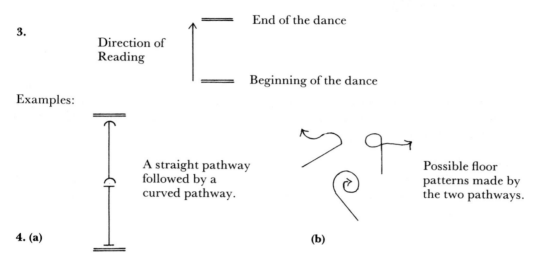

3.

Direction of Reading

End of the dance

Beginning of the dance

Examples:

A straight pathway followed by a curved pathway.

Possible floor patterns made by the two pathways.

4. (a)

(b)

The pathways may begin at any point in the room and facing any direction. They will take the same length of time to perform.

Developing Travelling Patterns

Travelling patterns can be developed by changing the design, by varying the timing, by being specific about the type and aim of the pathway you make, where you are facing in the room and in which area of the room you are dancing; by selecting a particular direction, number, level and size of steps made on a chosen pathway.

Time

If you wish to change how long the pathway takes to perform you change the length of the symbol. The duration of the movement is shown by the length of the symbol, a long symbol indicates a slow movement and a short symbol indicates a quick movement.

Examples:

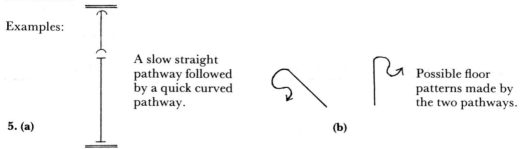

A slow straight pathway followed by a quick curved pathway.

Possible floor patterns made by the two pathways.

5. (a)

(b)

You may start at any point in the room and facing any direction. The straight pathway must take longer to perform than the curved pathway.

Space

If you wish to state the length of the pathway, the distance, you add the symbols for extension and contraction.

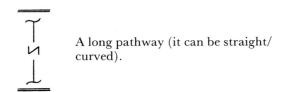

Ⅳ	Extend	✕	Contract
6. Ⅳ	Extend further	✳	Contract further

The extension and contraction symbols are placed within the pathway symbol. This will change the size of steps you make as you travel.

The extension symbol indicates that you cover more ground, i.e., that the pathway must be longer than normal or you may take longer or more steps to travel further.

Example:

7.   A long pathway (it can be straight/curved).

The contraction symbol indicates that you cover less ground, i.e., that the pathway must be shorter than normal or you may take shorter or fewer steps to travel less.

Example:

8.   A short pathway (it can be straight/curved).

Example:

9.   A long slow straight pathway followed by a short pathway circling either right or left.

Circular Pathways

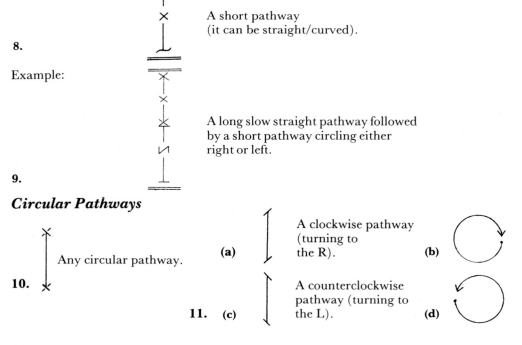

10.   Any circular pathway.

(a)   A clockwise pathway (turning to the R). **(b)**

11. **(c)**   A counterclockwise pathway (turning to the L). **(d)**

Amount of circling — parts of a circle

A black pin is placed inside the pathway sign to show how much you have turned, i.e., how much you have changed front.

Where you start is like the number twelve on a clock and the black pins are the hands of the clock moving clockwise and counterclockwise.

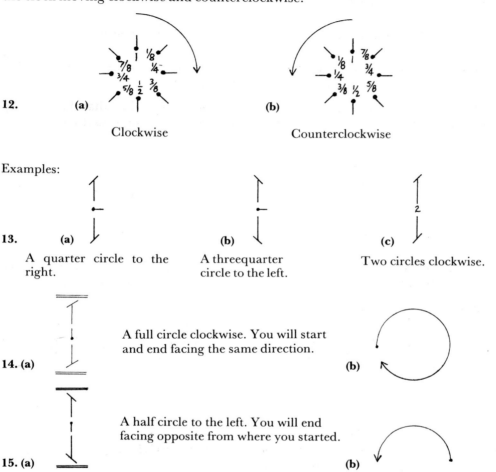

12.   **(a)**   **(b)**

Clockwise   Counterclockwise

Examples:

13.   **(a)**   **(b)**   **(c)**

A quarter circle to the right.

A threequarter circle to the left.

Two circles clockwise.

14. (a)   A full circle clockwise. You will start and end facing the same direction.   **(b)**

15. (a)   A half circle to the left. You will end facing opposite from where you started.   **(b)**

The following pathway is made up of two half circles the first clockwise and the second counterclockwise.

Dancer begins first half circle.

Dancer begins second half circle.

16. (a)   **(b)**

Facing in the Room

The dancer makes a certain design on the floor and faces specific points in the room as he or she performs the movements and pathways given. These changes of front are indicated on the score by the use of front signs.

Front signs:

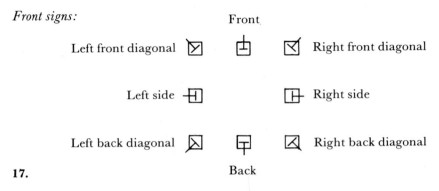

17.

The front signs are placed on the left side of the staff.

Examples:

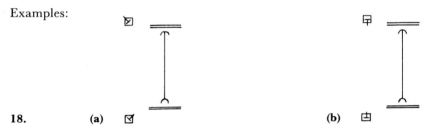

18. **(a)** ☑

Start facing the right front diagonal, perform a curved path and end facing left front diagonal.

(b) 凸

Start facing the front and at the end of a curved path face the back of the room.

Floor Plans

A floor plan illustrating the starting and finishing positions and the design of the pathways is usually given with the notated score. This will help the dancer to find the correct placement.

Room or Stage Area

The room or stage is represented by an open rectangle.

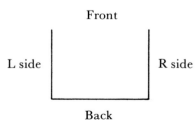

19.

Indication of the Performer

The dancer's location in the room or stage area is indicated by the use of pins and wedges. The pins, ↳ = a girl and ↓ = a boy, show the dancer's starting position. The wedges, Δ = a girl and ▲ = a boy, show the dancer's finishing position. The point of the pin and wedge indicates the direction in which the dancer is facing.

Indication of the Pathway

A path across the floor of the room and stage area is indicated on the floor plan by the use of an arrow. This shows the progression from the starting point.

20.

The dancer makes a half circular path, ending to face the back of the room.

Example:

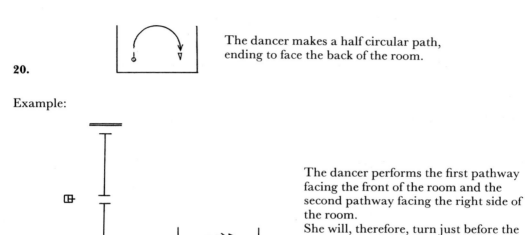

The dancer performs the first pathway facing the front of the room and the second pathway facing the right side of the room.
She will, therefore, turn just before the beginning of the second pathway.
Forward steps are understood in this example.

21.

Specific Areas of the Room

The room area signs indicate in which area of the room a dancer is performing.

Room Area Signs

Front

Left front corner ◪   ▭   ◩ Right front corner

Centre

Left side ▯   ◈   ▯ Right side

Left back corner ◣   ▭   ◪ Right back corner

Back

22.

Example:

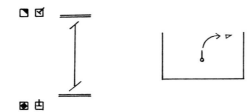

The dancer starts in centre of the room, facing front. She performs a clockwise circular pathway to end in the right front corner of the room, facing the right front diagonal.

23.

In a dance where there are many pathways several floor plans may be needed.

Example:

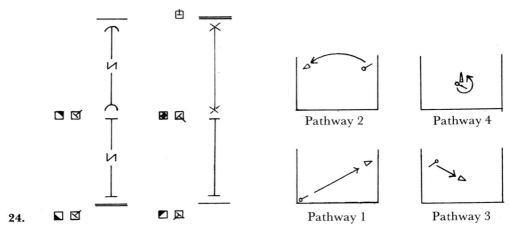

Pathway 2

Pathway 4

Pathway 1

Pathway 3

24.

Aims of a Pathway

The aim of a pathway may be for the dancer to move towards, away from or to reach another dancer, object or part of the room.

$$\bigvee = \text{Towards} \qquad \bigwedge = \text{Away}$$

25.　　**(a)**　　　　　　　　　　　　　　　**(b)**

When a dancer makes a movement towards another dancer, an object or part of the room, the appropriate sign for the dancer and object or part of the room is placed with the 'towards' symbol.

Examples:

26.　　**(a)**　　　　　　　　　　　　　**(b)**

Make a movement towards a partner.

Make a movement towards the front of the room.

When a dancer moves away from another dancer, an object or a part of the room, the appropriate sign is placed within the 'away' symbol.

Examples:

27.　(a)

Make a movement away from partner.

(b)

Make a movement away from the left front corner.

Advancing and Retreating

When the 'toward' and 'away' symbols are used with pathway symbols the dancer travels towards/approaches or moves away/retreats from another dancer, object or part of the room.

The dancer may or may not arrive at or leave completely the specified point.

Examples:

28.　(a)

A dancer travels on a straight path towards the centre of the room.

(b)

A dancer travels on a curved path away from the front of the room.

Arriving

When a dancer reaches a specific point, i.e., either a person, object or place in the room, the indication is written at the end of a path symbol and tied to it with a small vertical bow.

Examples:

29.　(a)

Travel on a straight pathway, arriving at the front of the room.

(b)

Travel on a curved path, to arrive with your partner.

Direction and Pathways
The standard system of direction

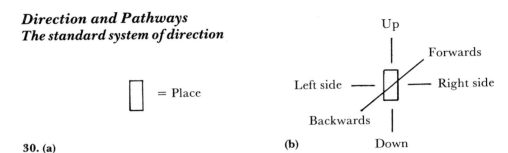

30. (a) = Place **(b)**

Place is centred in the dancer and so travels with you all the time.

Direction is related to 'place', i.e., forwards is always in front of you; backwards is always behind you; right side is to your right; left side is to your left side; up is always to the sky and down is always to the floor. Therefore, the direction forward is determined by where you are facing and up and down remain constant.

Symbols for the eight main directions are modifications of the basic symbol – 'place' – and the shapes are pictorial in pointing to the direction they describe.

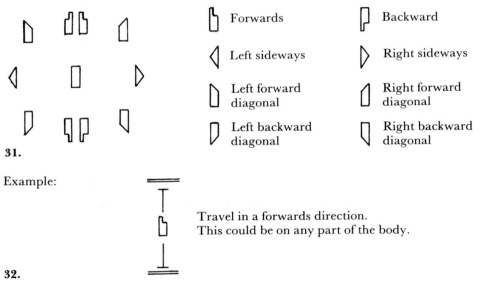

31.

Example:

Travel in a forwards direction.
This could be on any part of the body.

32.

Steps and Pathways
To specify steps whilst making a pathway the symbol ⫪ for supporting on the feet is placed together with the appropriate direction symbol within the pathway symbol.

Examples:

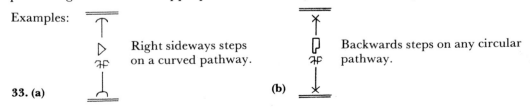

Right sideways steps on a curved pathway.

Backwards steps on any circular pathway.

33. (a)   **(b)**

Number of Steps

The number of steps whilst making a pathway may be indicated by placing the number together with the symbol for supporting and the direction symbol. They may be written within the pathway or within a bow placed at the side of the pathway.

Examples:

34.   (a)   (b)   (c)

Four backward steps on a curved pathway.

Eight right forward diagonal steps on a straight pathway.

Six forward steps on a clockwise circular pathway.

Level of Steps

The level of steps is indicated by shading in the direction symbol.

Low level   *Middle level*   *High level*

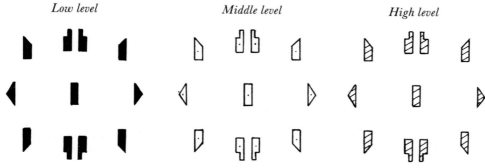

35. **(a)** Lowered steps, stepping with knees bent.

(b) Normal, horizontal walking level.

(c) Lifted, stepping on half toes with straight legs.

Examples:

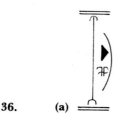

36.   (a)   (b)   (c)

Whilst travelling on a curved pathway, step sideways with knees bent.

Whilst travelling on any chosen pathway, take forward middle level steps.

Whilst travelling on a straight pathway step backwards at a high level.

Size of Steps

The size of steps is indicated by placing the extension symbols и , и and the contractions symbols ✕ , ✳ before the direction symbol.

Examples:

37. (a)  (b) 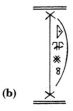 (c)

Long forward low steps on a straight pathway.

Eight very small right sideways middle level steps on a circular pathway.

Four very long forward steps at middle level to make a complete clockwise circle.

PRACTICE IN READING AND WRITING

P. 1. Dance the following pathways:

(a)   (b) (c)

P. 2. Dance and notate the following patterns:

(a) a long curved pathway followed by two short straight pathways.
(b) a long circular pathway followed by a long straight pathway.
(c) two short pathways followed by one long pathway.

P. 3. Dance and notate some patterns of your own. Draw the pathway you have made and state what step patterns you made on the pathway.

P. 4. Perform the following sequence of pathways and complete the floor plan. What kind of pathway is it?

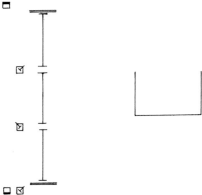

P. 5.

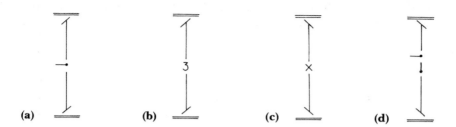

(i)   Try out the above circular pathways.
(ii) Draw the pathway you have made and state where you faced at the beginning and end of the pathway.
(iii) What movements did you select to make the pathway? Write them down by the side of the pathway symbol.

P. 6.   Dance and notate the following patterns:

  (a) Facing the front of the room, perform two short pathways and one long pathway, ending facing the right side of the room. Indicate where you are facing throughout.
  (b) Facing the right front diagonal, perform a pathway which ends facing the left back diagonal.

P. 7.

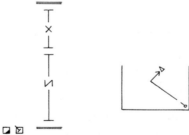

What size and direction of steps will the dancer perform in the above example.

P. 8.   Notate the following pathways and indicate where the dancer is facing on each pathway.

P. 9.   Notate the pathways and floor plan from a dance you know.

P. 10. Experiment with the movement ideas of 'approaching', 'retreating' and 'arriving'. Notate your dance patterns.

P. 11.(a)   Read and dance the following examples:

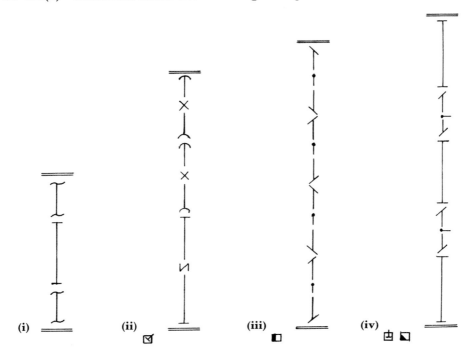

(i)   (ii)   (iii)   (iv)

(b)   Describe what is happening in each example, considering:

(i)   the type of steps you chose to perform in each dance pattern.
(ii)   the number, size and level of the steps you made in each dance pattern.
(iii)   the design you made on the floor. Draw the floor plans.
(iv)   where you started and ended in each dance pattern.
(v)   where you were facing at the beginning, during and at the end of each dance pattern.

P. 12.   The following extract is taken from the ballet 'Echoi II' by Jaap Flier. The ballet is in the repertoire of the Ballet Rambert and was first danced by members of the company in 1979. The music for this section is 'Echoi II' composed by Lukas Voss.
The extract is the opening section of the ballet and is danced by a boy and a girl. Here the notation gives a general indication of the movement and only the dance of the boy is recorded. As the book progresses more specific detail of the movement of both dancers is given.

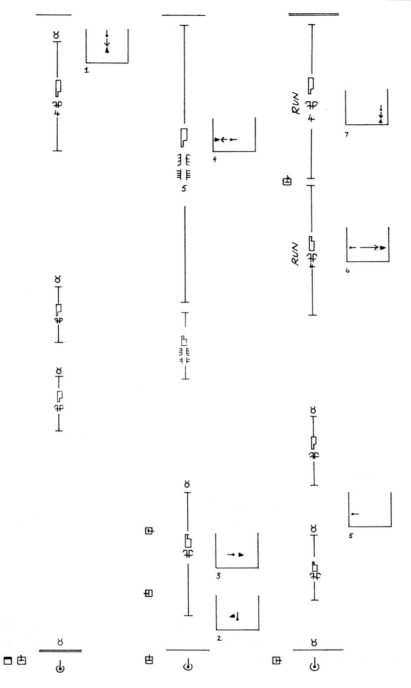

𝄖 = supporting on hands and knees

𝄖 = supporting on hands and feet

⍐ = stillness

Part 2

Partner and group relationship

Dancing with a partner

Partners may approach, meet, move together, part, dance near, by the side of, behind or in front of each other; lead, follow, move together, in canon or in opposition; address, touch, support, surround, grasp, carry each other or an object.

Each dancer is usually given a separate staff which are joined together by a line at the start of each page. In the following example dancer A begins in the L back corner, B in the R front corner; they approach each other on straight pathways, both ending in the centre of the room area.

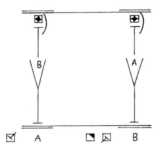 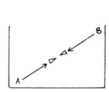

38.

The Meeting Line

During a dance the relationship of one dancer to another may change. This change of relationship is indicated by the use of the meeting line. The meeting line is a stroke placed on the right side of the staff and indicates that a dancer meets another dancer at that moment. If the relationship of the dancers remains the same throughout the dance the meeting line is placed below the staff.

|P   Partner is to the right.

P| Partner is to the left.

P   Partner is in front.

P   Partner is behind.

P   Partner is diagonally left in front.

P   Partner is diagonally right in front.

P   Partner is diagonally right behind.

P   Partner is diagonally left behind.

39.

Examples of partner relationships:

Meeting and parting   *Matching*

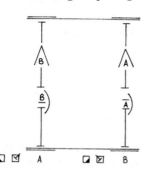   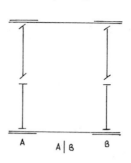

40. **(a)**   **(b)**

Both A and B perform straight paths to arrive with B in front of A. They then travel away from each other.

A and B dance together side by side throughout the dance.

Contrasting   *Leading and following*

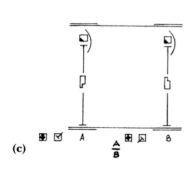   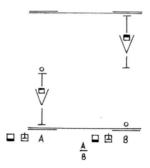

(c)   **(d)**

A and B facing each other arrive in the L back corner of the stage; A making backward steps and B making forward steps.

A is in front of B, both facing front; they move in canon towards the front of the stage, A leading B.

Addressing

When relating to someone or something by gesturing/signalling/etc., the addressing symbol is used. A horizontal line is drawn from the staff of the active person and within the cup is placed the person or object which is being addressed.

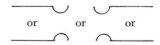

or   or   or

41.

Examples:

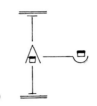

42.   **(a)**   **(b)**

The dancer travels on a straight path and at the end of the pathway addresses a partner.

The dancer leaves the front of the room area whilst addressing the front of the room area.

Nearness

When a dancer is near another dancer or an object, this nearness is indicated by a dotted horizontal bow ╲ ＿ ＿ ╱ or ╱ ￣ ￣ ╲ .

Example:

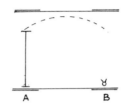

43.

४ = remain quiet, hold.

A travels on a straight path ending near to B.

Touching

When a dancer touches another dancer or an object this contact is indicated by using a horizontal bow ╲＿╱ or ╱￣╲ .

Example:

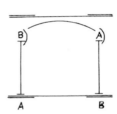

A & B travel to each other and touch.

44.

Supporting

When a dancer supports another dancer or an object the symbol ╲ or ╱ for supporting is used.

The dancer or object which is supporting is written at the lower end of the sign and the dancer or object which is being supported is written at the upper end.

Example:

A travels on a straight path supporting a box.

45.

Surrounding

When a movement encloses or surrounds, the contraction symbol × is added to the bow ˋ ˎ ˎₓ ˎ ˊ ˊ . The × within the bow is placed nearer the active part.

Example:

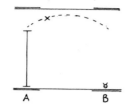

A travels on a straight path, arriving and enclosing B.

46.

Grasping

When the contraction symbol × is placed within the contact bow ⌣ₓ⌣ , a grasping action results. The × within the bow is placed nearer the active part, i.e., the part which is doing the grasping.

Examples:

47.

⅏ Both hands

ʅ Right hand

ʃ Left hand

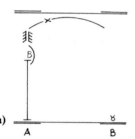

48.   (a)

A approaches B and with both hands grasps B. (The × is placed nearer A as A does the grasping).

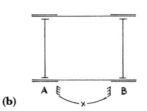

(b)

Holding hands A and B travel together on a straight path. (It is equal grasping as the × is placed in the centre).

Holding

When the dancer holds and carries the weight of another dancer or an object, the contraction sign × is placed within the symbol for supporting, ⌣×⌐ or ⌐×⌣ . The × within the bow is placed nearer the active part.

Example:

The dancer holds and carries a walking stick.

49.

Group Formations

Pre-staff information
Certain information is written below each staff to explain:

      (i) who is to perform the dance.
     (ii) the relationship of one dancer to another.
    (iii) how many people are in the dance.
    (iv) where the dancers are to perform on the stage.

We have seen how to indicate dancers on a floor plan in Part 1. Any identification selected to identify the dancers must be maintained throughout the score.

Indications of people
In many dances we identify the performers as a couple, trio or within a numbered group. The number and sex of the dancer/s are indicated by the placing of the appropriate pin/s, enclosed in a circle, before the staff.

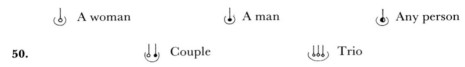

    A woman   A man   Any person

50.   Couple   Trio

A double circle represents each person or each group.

    Each person   Each man   Each woman

51.   Each couple   Each trio

Examples:

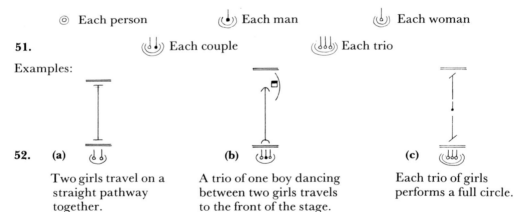

52. **(a)**   **(b)**   **(c)**

(a)	(b)	(c)
Two girls travel on a straight pathway together.	A trio of one boy dancing between two girls travels to the front of the stage.	Each trio of girls performs a full circle.

Relationship of one group to another
We have seen earlier how to indicate the relationship of one dancer to another by using the meeting line.

Example:

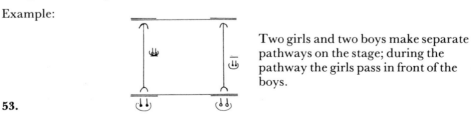

Two girls and two boys make separate pathways on the stage; during the pathway the girls pass in front of the boys.

53.

Indentification of particular dancers

Dancers who have a distinct part to play throughout a dance are usually shown in the score by a choice of letters of the alphabet.

Each dancer is given an identifying letter and this is maintained throughout the score.

Example: A = girl in the red costume
B = boy in the orange costume
C = girl in the yellow costume
D = boy in the green costume
54. E = girl in the blue costume.

If they are dancing in unison only one staff need be used. On the floor plan only the letter is added to the pin as the pin distinguishes the boy and girl dancers.

Example:

All five dancers travel on a straight pathway to arrive in the left front corner of the stage.

55. A B C D E

If the dancers have different movements to perform in the dance, each dancer is given a separate staff.

Example:

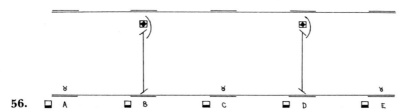

56. A   B   C   D   E

A, C, E stay still as B, D travel to the centre of the stage.

Number of people

In some dances the performers do not need to be specifically identified. It is satisfactory to identify them within a numbered group.

The sign for the number of people in the group is a small circle containing a number. If a group is named, this is also placed within a circle.

Examples:

57. **(a)**

Six girls in a group.

(b) A group called X with eight people in it.

(c) A group called Y with ten people in it, five boys and five girls.

Together with these indications of people, the front signs and room area signs (refer Part 1) are placed with the staffs to give clear information about who is dancing and where they begin on the stage.

Examples:

58.   (a)

A group of six dancers beginning in the left back corner of the stage.

(b)

Group A starts in the front corner, Group B in the centre and Group C in the right back corner of the stage; they all begin facing front.

Dancing in a line
The following pre-signs indicate the relationship of the dancers in a line formation:

59.

Side by side   In front of each other   Behind each other

Examples:

60.   (a) 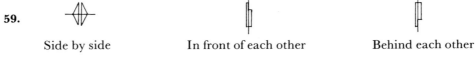   (b)

Five girls in a line side by side, facing front start at the back of the stage; they travel on a straight pathway with forward steps.

Three dancers one behind the other and facing the right front corner; start in the right front corner and travel with backward steps on a straight pathway.

(c)

Two groups of three dancers; dancers in each group side by side and facing front; Line A is in front of Line B; each dancer in Line A has one of the dancers in Line B behind her and to her right (right back diagonal relationship).

Dancing in a circle

When dancing in a circle the dancer relates to the centre of the circle and is aware of facing the centre, having his/her back to it or having his/her right or left side to it or having a diagonal relationship to it.

To indicate the dancer's relationship to the centre of the circle the focal point • is placed on the appropriate side of the meeting line (see page 26).

61.

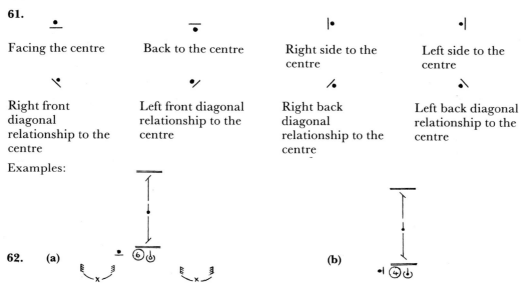

Facing the centre   Back to the centre   Right side to the   Left side to the
centre   centre

Right front   Left front diagonal   Right back   Left back diagonal
diagonal   relationship to the   diagonal   relationship to the
relationship to the   centre   relationship to the   centre
centre   centre

Examples:

62.   (a)

Six girls in a group, holding hands and facing the centre of the circle make a full clockwise circle; they will be making sideways steps.

(b)

Four boys in a group, with their left sides to the centre of the circle make a full circle counterclockwise; they will be making forward steps.

$\sim$ = release

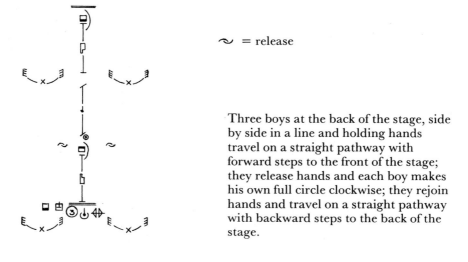

(c)

Three boys at the back of the stage, side by side in a line and holding hands travel on a straight pathway with forward steps to the front of the stage; they release hands and each boy makes his own full circle clockwise; they rejoin hands and travel on a straight pathway with backward steps to the back of the stage.

PRACTICE IN READING AND WRITING

P. 13.   Explain what is happening in the following patterns:

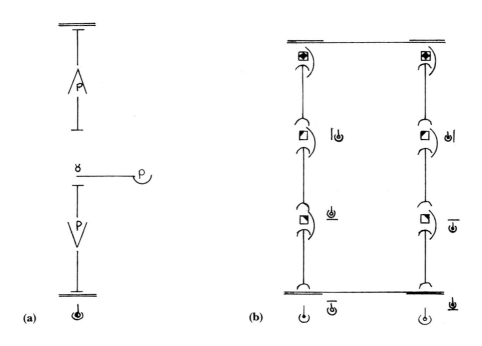

(a)

(b)

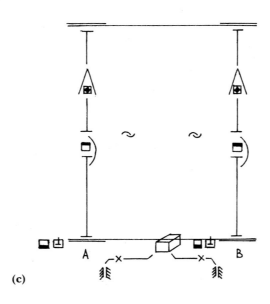

(c)

P. 14. Notate the following pattern:
Two dancers A and B start in the centre of the stage. B travels away to the right front corner of the stage and circles the stage clockwise. At each corner B addresses A, arriving back at the right front corner. A approaches B and leads B in a full clockwise circle around the room. They end facing each other in the right front corner of the stage.

P. 15. Read and dance the following dance pattern. Select a suitable piece of music and develop the dance pattern into a complete dance. Notate your dance.

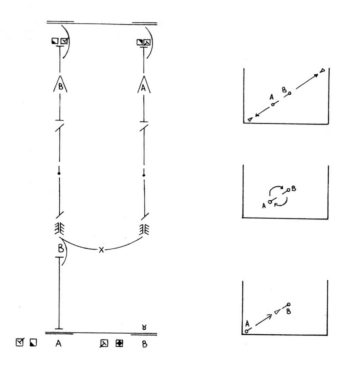

P. 16. Give the pre-staff information for the following group formations at the beginning of a dance:

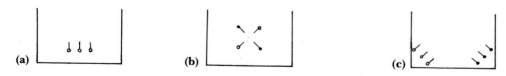

(a)   (b)   (c)

P. 17. Draw the floor plans for the following pre-staff information:

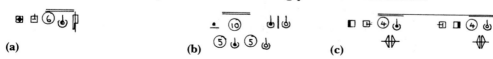

(a)   (b)   (c)

P. 18. Notate the following group movements. Dance the pattern and select your own ways of travelling:

(a) Three dancers, starting in the left back corner, travel in a straight line to the front of the stage.

(b) Four dancers, starting in the centre of the stage facing front and in a square formation, travel to the front of the stage; they then travel round the stage counterclockwise to end in their starting position; they repeat the same pattern to the other side.

P. 19. Read and dance the following dance pattern. Select a suitable piece of music and develop the dance pattern into a complete group dance.

Notate the dance you have composed.

ŏ = stillness

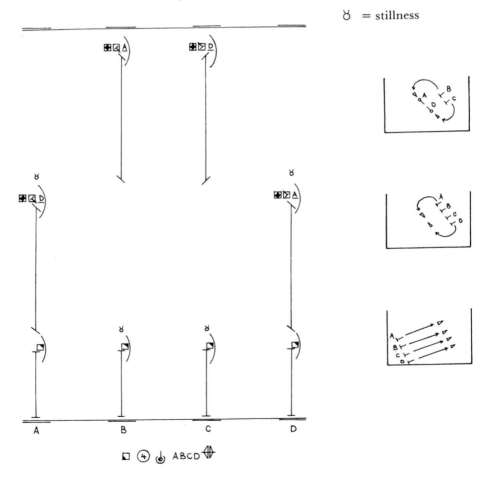

P. 20. (a) Compose and notate a dance which involves three or more dancers.

(b) Compose and notate a circle dance for four people.

(c) Compose and notate a dance involving changing group formations.

Part 3
Body action

Basic Actions of the Whole Body

63. **(a)** |

An action, this involves a transference of weight

(b) ୪

Stillness

(c) |

A gesture, this involves no transference of weight

Examples:

64. **(a)**

A slow action of the whole body followed by two quicker actions of the whole body.

(b)

Perform three quick actions pausing in between each action.

(c)

A gesture followed by an action, pause, another gesture and an action in faster timing.

The above phrases give a very general idea of movements and you are free to interpret them as you wish. More detail can be added about:

   (i)   the action performed.
  (ii)   the degree of extension or contraction.
(iii)   where and how the dancer travels in space.

Possible actions for the examples above could be notated by using the following symbols.

65. **(a)**

Any pathway (refer to Part 1 for more detail of pathways)

(b)

Any turn, rotation, revolution

(c)

Sink down

(d)

Rise

(e)

Jump

Examples:

66. **(a)** This sequence could be interpreted as the dancer performed a stretched gesture making a wide shape, followed by a sinking down. **(b)**

Notice that the timing has not changed i.e., the symbols are the same length. The extension symbol и is attached to the sign for a gesture, indicating the nature of the gesture.

Simultaneous and Successive Movements

When two or more actions happen at the same time, i.e., simultaneously, the symbols representing the actions are placed side by side.

Examples:

67. **(a)**

Jumping whilst turning.

(b)

Travel and revolve during the second half of the pathway.

When actions happen one after the other, i.e., successively, the symbols representing the actions are placed one after the other.

Examples:

68. **(a)**

Gesture then turn, pause, gesture, then turn.

(b)

Travel on a straight path, jump and sink down.

Use of Space

The extension and contraction signs change the amount of space used by the body.

Examples:

69. **(a)**

A very contracted action of the whole body e.g. a ball shape may be the result of such an action.

(b)

A very stretched action of the whole body e.g. a wide shape would result.

(c)

Travelling a long distance on a straight path.

Turning

70.

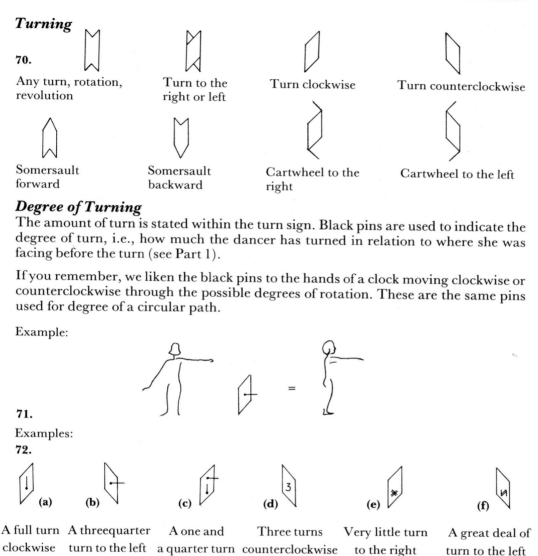

Any turn, rotation, revolution

Turn to the right or left

Turn clockwise

Turn counterclockwise

Somersault forward

Somersault backward

Cartwheel to the right

Cartwheel to the left

Degree of Turning

The amount of turn is stated within the turn sign. Black pins are used to indicate the degree of turn, i.e., how much the dancer has turned in relation to where she was facing before the turn (see Part 1).

If you remember, we liken the black pins to the hands of a clock moving clockwise or counterclockwise through the possible degrees of rotation. These are the same pins used for degree of a circular path.

Example:

71.

Examples:

72.

(a) A full turn clockwise

(b) A threequarter turn to the left

(c) A one and a quarter turn to the right

(d) Three turns counterclockwise

(e) Very little turn to the right

(f) A great deal of turn to the left

Twisting

Twist within part of the body. The hold sign o is added to the base of the turn sign to show that a part of the body (usually the base) is held and does not rotate.

A clockwise twist

A counterclockwise twist

Actions of parts of the body

To indicate an action of a particular body part, place the sign for that part of the body before the action symbol.

Joint Signs

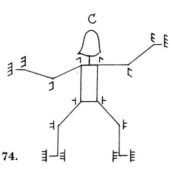

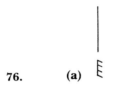

74.

Arms		Legs	
⌐	shoulder	┤├	hip
⅃ Ⅎ	elbow	⅃ Ⅎ	knee
⅃ Ⅎ	wrist	⅃ Ⅎ	ankle
⅃ Ⅎ	hand	⅃ Ⅎ	foot
75. ⅃ Ⅎ	fingers	⅃ Ⅎ	toes
left right		left right	

Examples:

76.   **(a)**

Action of the right hand.

(b)

The head turns a little to the right.

(c)

The right shoulder lifts up.

Limbs

77.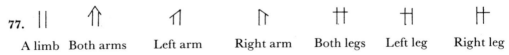

A limb   Both arms   Left arm   Right arm   Both legs   Left leg   Right leg

Parts of a Limb

The part of the limb which is to be moved is that part above the joint sign.

Examples:

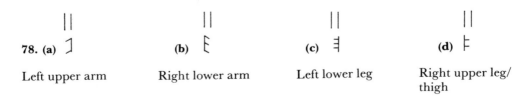

78. (a)
Left upper arm

(b)
Right lower arm

(c)
Left lower leg

(d)
Right upper leg/ thigh

Body Areas

 is the basic sign for an area. The actual body area is indicated by placing the symbol for that body part within the □ .

79.

| Area of head | Shoulder section | Waist | Chest | Pelvis | Torso |

Body Surfaces

⊓ is the basic sign for a surface. By placing the tick on a specific side of the ⊓, a surface is indicated.

80.

| Face | Right side of the waist | Left side of the pelvis | Back of the torso |

Examples:

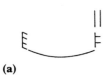

(a)

The right hand touches
the right upper leg.

(b)

Hands touch the face.

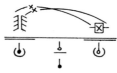

(c)

The boy grasps the girl
by the waist, right hand
to right side and left
hand to left side of waist.

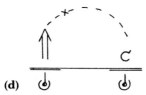

(d)

A dancer surrounds
another dancer's head
with his/her arms.

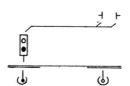

(e)

A girl sits on a boy's
back.

81.

PRACTICE IN READING AND WRITING

P. 21. Read and dance the following patterns. Select an appropriate piece of music and use these patterns as a starting point for a dance.

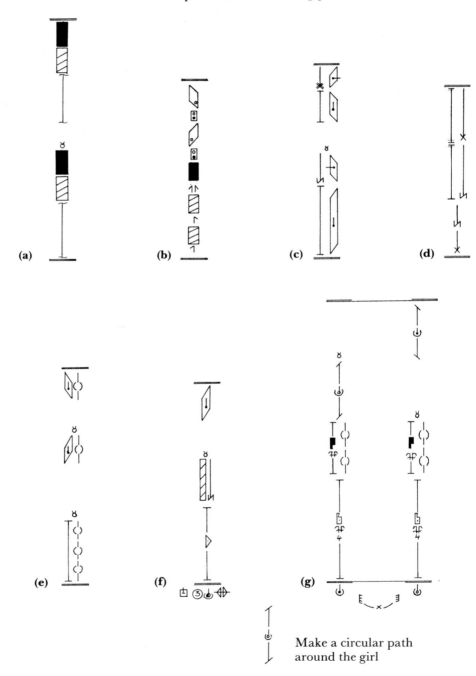

(a) (b) (c) (d)

(e) (f) (g)

Make a circular path
around the girl

P. 22. (a) Notate the following partner situations:

      (i) grasping wrists.
      (ii) leaning back to back.
      (iii) holding a partner by the waist.
      (iv) touching the face with the fingertips.
      (v) tapping one's own thighs, then clap hands with a partner.

     (b) (i) Notate a dance sequence during which two dancers hold hands.
        (ii) Notate a dance you have composed during which the dancers support each others weight.
        (iii) Notate a dance which shows a dancer caring for another, for example, a mother caring for her child.
        (iv) Compose and notate a dance in which dancers show contrasting movements, for example, a dance demonstrating an argument between two people.
        (v) Compose and notate a dance in which the partners dance in harmony, for example, a dance about friendship.

P. 23. Extract from the ballet 'Echoi' choreographed by Jaap Flier.

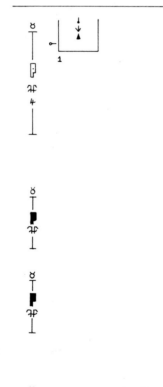

                                    = off stage

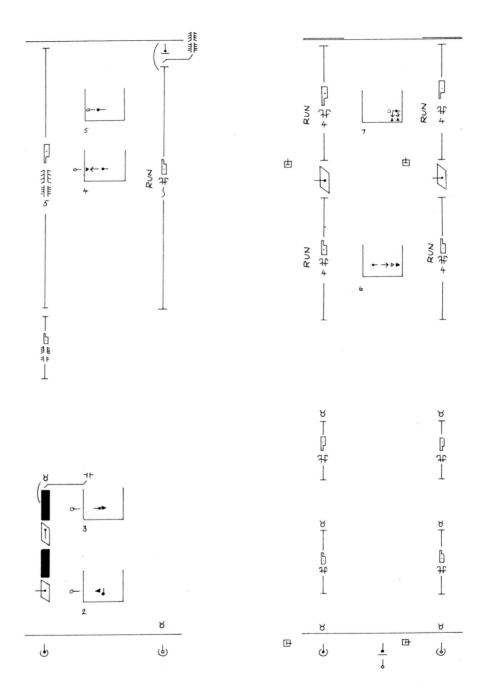

Part 4
The vertical staff & timing

In the previous parts we have been involved in the general description of what has been happening in the body. We were allowed a certain amount of freedom in the interpretation of the movement patterns. If we wish to be more specific about the patterns we dance we can use the vertical staff.

The Centre Line

We often wish to indicate actions occurring on one side of the body or the other. To show this the vertical line is drawn from the double starting line to represent the vertical centre line in the body, i.e., the spine.

82.　(a)　L　R　　　　　　　　　　(b)

Right is on the right side of the Centre Line, left is on the left, (as you face the paper).

Example:

83.　(a)　　　　　　　　　　　　(b)

Actions of the right and left side of the body.

One long forward movement at middle level of the right side of the body.

The Staff

The staff is a vertical three line staff. The staff represents the body, the centre line being the centre line of the body, dividing the right side from the left.

Vertical columns on each side of the centre line are used for the main parts of the body. Movements of the legs and feet are written within the three line staff.

Movements of the torso, arms and head are written outside the three line staff.

84.　(a)　　　　　　　　　　　　(b)

Three Line Staff

To show a movement of a particular body part the movement indication is written within the appropriate vertical column.

Example:

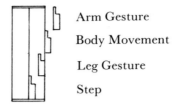

Arm Gesture

Body Movement

Leg Gesture

Step

85. Forward movements of the right side of the body.

Use of Columns

Supports

Supports are written in the first column. Symbols placed in these columns indicate movement progression of the whole body while supporting on the feet. Weight can be taken on any part of the body but it is assumed that the dancer is stepping on the feet unless the sign for a body part is written before a symbol.

Example:

86. (a)

Four forward steps starting on the right foot.

(b)

Four forward steps on the hands, starting on the right hand.

Thus supporting on the feet is written on either side of the centre line. By placing the direction symbol on the right side of the centre line, or on the left side, or on both sides we show that weight is on the right foot, the left foot or both feet. Weight on one foot is cancelled by a step on the other foot.

Place

 = Place

Place is the centre point. For supports it is underneath you. When on one foot, place is under that foot. For feet together place is between the feet.

87.

Examples:

88. (a)

Standing on the right foot.

(b)

Standing on the left foot.

(c)

Standing on both feet.

Stepping in Different Directions

To indicate that steps are being made in certain directions, the appropriate direction symbols are used.

(Refer – 'Steps and Pathways' – The Standard System of Direction in Part 2)

Examples:

  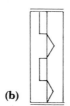 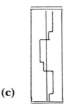

89.   **(a)**   **(b)**   **(c)**

Four Steps forward.   Step side and close,   Three Backward steps.
                          repeat.

Relationship of feet whilst stepping

The relationship of one foot to the other when stepping is shown by the use of the black pins.

$\downarrow$ = in front of

90. $\uparrow$ = behind

When making sideways steps the foot needs to cross in front or behind the other foot.

Example:

Four sideways steps to the left. On the second step the right foot crosses in front of the left foot; on the fourth step the right foot crosses behind the left.

91.

Step and close

When bringing the feet together, one foot is often closed in front or behind the other foot.

Examples:

92.   **(a)**   **(b)**

Left foot closes in front of   Four steps on the spot, the
the right foot.   feet stepping directly behind
                                     each other. This will produce
                                     a slight travelling backwards.

47

Walking on the centre line

In normal walking each foot is placed in its own track. This track relates to the hip of that leg and the centre line of the body. Walking on the centre line, i.e., one foot in front of the other, as in tightrope walking can be shown as in example (b).

Examples:

93.   (a)

Normal walking

(b)

Tightrope walking

Levels of Support

When supporting on the legs, flexion of the legs and the part of the foot on which the weight is being supported, can be indicated. There are three main levels: middle, low and high.

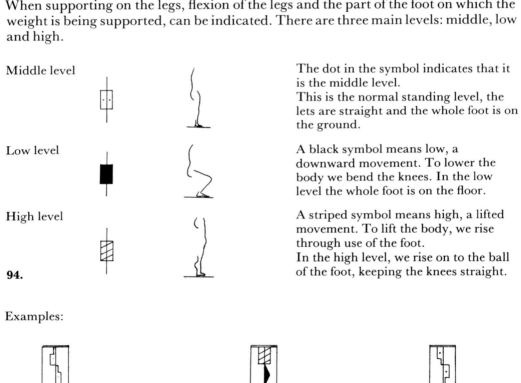

Middle level

The dot in the symbol indicates that it is the middle level.
This is the normal standing level, the lets are straight and the whole foot is on the ground.

Low level

A black symbol means low, a downward movement. To lower the body we bend the knees. In the low level the whole foot is on the floor.

High level

A striped symbol means high, a lifted movement. To lift the body, we rise through use of the foot.
In the high level, we rise on to the ball of the foot, keeping the knees straight.

94.

Examples:

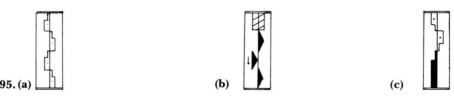

95. (a)

Four Steps forward at middle level.

(b)

Three deep level steps to the right, left foot crossing in front of right, then closing feet together at high level.

(c)

A forward step in low level followed by two quick middle level backward steps.

Size of steps

Steps are the dancer's own normal step length unless an extension И or contraction X sign is added. These are placed before the appropriate direction symbol and indicate that a step is longer or shorter than normal.

Examples:

96.

(a)

Two medium level forward steps at normal step length.

(b)

Three small steps sideways high.

(c)

A long low level step backwards, then closing feet together at high level.

Steps and Pathways

To indicate that a specific path is made as you perform certain steps the pathway symbol accompanies the steps and is placed on the right hand side of the staff. If you need the additional information regarding where the dancer is facing and in which area of the stage she is dancing, it is shown by placing the front signs and room area signs on the left hand side of the staff.

Example:

97.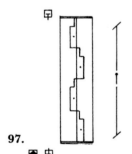

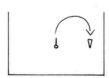

Starting in the centre and facing the front of the stage, perform four forward steps making a half circle clockwise to end facing the back of the room.

Use of the hold sign

When the hold sign is used in the support column, it indicates that weight is to be held on that foot. If weight is to be held on both feet, the hold sign can be centred over both symbols.

98.

(a)

Keep the weight on the right as the left closes.

(b) *or*

Hold the weight on both feet.

General Timing

In the previous parts we have been concerned only with a general indication of time. The relative length of a symbol indicates the duration of the movements, i.e., the longer the symbol the longer it takes to complete the movement and the shorter the symbol the sooner the movement is completed.

Measured Timing

The centre line of the vertical staff is also the time line.

In music, time is often divided into regular beats and these beats are organised into groups by using bar lines. In notation, the time line is divided into regular beats and bars to correspond with the accompanying music.

The measurement of the regular beat in the bar is indicated by marking the centre line of the staff at regular intervals with short horizontal strokes. Each short stroke shows the beginning of a new beat and the space between the strokes represents the length of the beat.

The staff is also marked off in bars by horizontal lines drawn across the staff.

Double horizontal lines indicate the beginning of the dance. Any indication before this double line signifies a starting position.

Double horizontal lines indicate the ending of the dance.

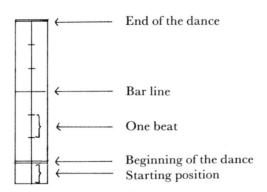

End of the dance

Bar line

One beat

Beginning of the dance
Starting position

99.

Numbering the beats and bars

If the counts for the beats are needed, they are numbered and placed outside the staff to the left just after the strokes indicating the beats.

The number for each bar is placed outside the beat numbers and directly after the bar line. These numbers are written larger than the beat numbers and should correspond with the numbered bars in the music score.

Simple Metres

The following examples illustrate the division of bars into equal units of time. The time signature is written to the left of the staff.

It is not always necessary to number the bars and beats.

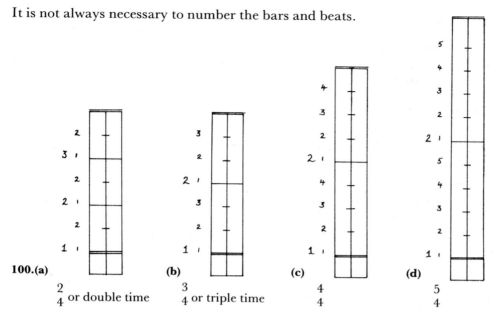

100.(a)   **(b)**   **(c)**   **(d)**

$\frac{2}{4}$ or double time $\frac{3}{4}$ or triple time $\frac{4}{4}$ $\frac{5}{4}$

Compound Metres

In compound time each main beat is divisible by 3. The compound time of $\frac{6}{8}$ is the most familiar but you may come across $\frac{9}{8}$, $\frac{12}{8}$, $\frac{6}{4}$ and $\frac{9}{4}$.

The $\frac{6}{8}$ is usually compared to a $\frac{2}{4}$ as there are two main beats in each bar.

Examples:

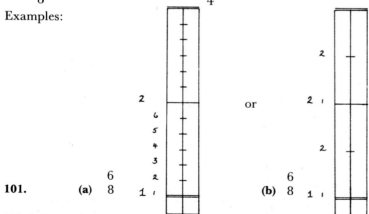

101.   **(a)** $\frac{6}{8}$ or   **(b)** $\frac{6}{8}$

Division of a Beat

As in music, the single beat is specified by a number 1, 2, 3, etc., depending on the number of beats in a bar. If the beat is divided in half, the first part is still called by its number and the second half is called 'x'. If the beat is divided into fours, the beat is counted '1, y, κ, u', the 'y' being pronounced as in 'any' and the 'u' as in 'up'.

102.   1 beat

Examples:

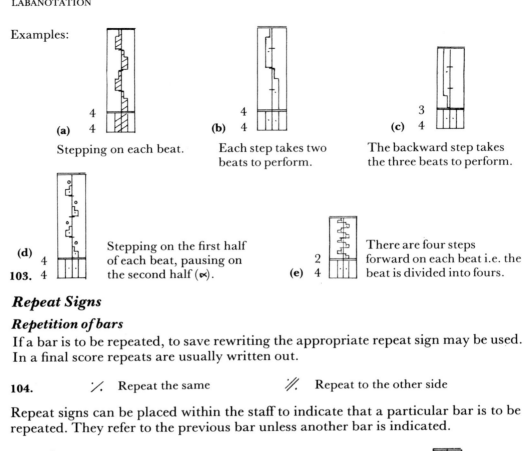

(a) $\frac{4}{4}$ — Stepping on each beat.

(b) $\frac{4}{4}$ — Each step takes two beats to perform.

(c) $\frac{3}{4}$ — The backward step takes the three beats to perform.

(d) $\frac{4}{4}$

103. — Stepping on the first half of each beat, pausing on the second half (⋈).

(e) $\frac{2}{4}$ — There are four steps forward on each beat i.e. the beat is divided into fours.

Repeat Signs

Repetition of bars

If a bar is to be repeated, to save rewriting the appropriate repeat sign may be used. In a final score repeats are usually written out.

104.   ∶⁄.   Repeat the same   ∶⁄⁄.   Repeat to the other side

Repeat signs can be placed within the staff to indicate that a particular bar is to be repeated. They refer to the previous bar unless another bar is indicated.

Examples:

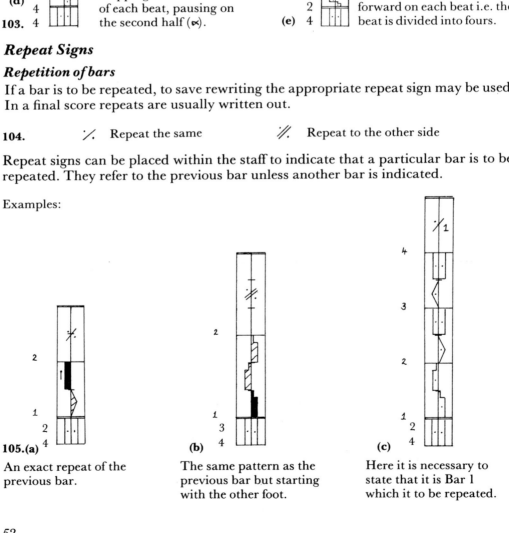

105.(a) An exact repeat of the previous bar.

(b) The same pattern as the previous bar but starting with the other foot.

(c) Here it is necessary to state that it is Bar 1 which it to be repeated.

Repetition of sections

If a pattern involving several bars is to be repeated, the repeat signs are modified so that they are horizontal ÷ and ÷ .

They are placed at the beginning on the left and at the end on the right of the section to be repeated.

Example:

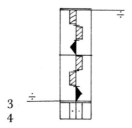

The pattern is danced twice.

106. 3/4

If the section of a dance is to be repeated more than twice, the number of times is written.

Example:

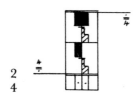

The pattern is danced alternately right then left
(four times in all).

107. 2/4

Longer Sectional repeats

If longer sections of a dance contain short repeats, the extended lines are made longer and bent to enclose the whole section.

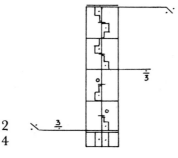

Two bars are danced three times,
followed by two bars not repeated.
The eight bars are repeated again.

108. 2/4

PRACTICE IN READING AND WRITING

P. 24. Read and dance the following patterns.

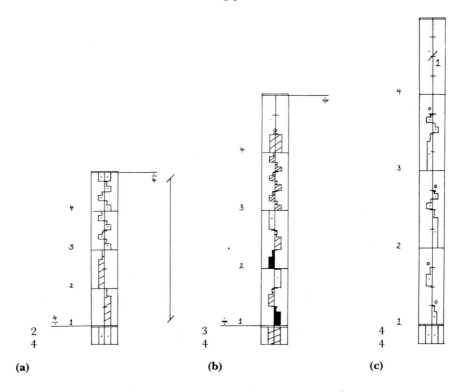

(a) (b) (c)

P. 25. Select a piece of music with a marching tempo and dance the following pattern.

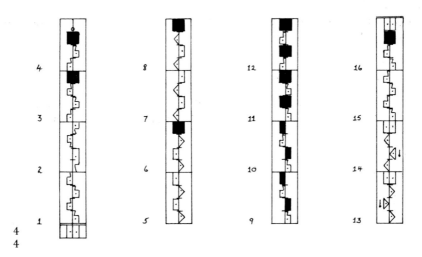

P. 26.   Try the following pattern to a waltz.

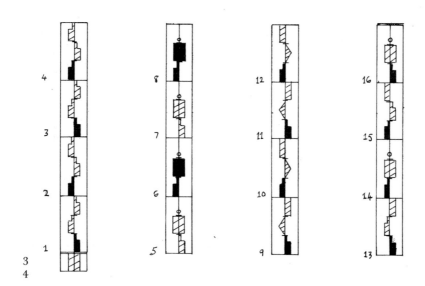

P. 27.   (a)   Compose and notate a dance where the music you had selected made you think of peace, war, happiness or sadness.

(b)   Selecting a quiet piece of music compose and notate a solo dance.

(c)   Select a piece of music which has contrasting moods within it. Compose and notate a group dance.

Part 5

Gestures of the body

A gesture of the whole body or body part is an action of that part which involves no transference of weight. Gestures are described as the point in space to which the extremity of the limb moves and are written in the vertical columns on each side of the centre line of the staff (see Part 4 'The Vertical Staff').

Gestures of the Legs and Arms

A gesture of the leg is written in the column for the leg. The direction of the leg is judged from the hip and the appropriate direction symbol is placed in the leg gesture column to indicate whether the leg is forwards, sideways or backwards of the hip.

Direction and Level

Low Level Leg Gestures – these are movements of the leg which are below hip level, slanting downward.

Example:

109.

Middle Level Leg Gestures – these are horizontal movements of the leg which are level with the hip joint.

Example:

110.

High Level Leg Gestures – these are movements of the leg which are above hip level, slanting upwards.

Example:

111.

56

Examples:

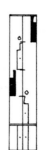

112.   **(a)**

Standing on the left leg
at middle level the right
leg moves forward
through low, middle then
high level.

(b)

Standing on the left leg,
the right leg swings
forward middle then
under the hip to
backward middle level.

(c)

Step on the right foot and
then whilst holding the
weight on the right foot,
gesture forward deep
with the left foot; perform
the same pattern on the
other side.

Touch with Parts of the Feet.

As we have seen in Part 2, contact between two dancers and a dancer with an
object is indicated by the use of the horizontal bow.

Touching the floor with specific parts of the foot whilst stepping or gesturing at a low
level is indicated by using small upward and downward hooks ⤵⤴ .

These hooks are derived from the horizontal bow ⌣ and represent particular
parts of the feet.

113.

Examples:

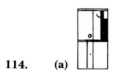

114.   **(a)**

Standing on the left foot
the right foot is extended
forward low with toe
touching the floor.

(b)

Standing with feet
together touch the floor
to the left side with the
left foot, first with the toe
then with the heel.

(c)

Walking forwards on the
heels.

Sliding

The indication that the foot is sliding across the floor is shown by using two hooks. This may be for a sliding step or a sliding gesture.

Examples:

115.   **(a)**   **(b)**   **(c)**

Slide on the toe to the right side, then step on the right foot.

Sliding steps on the whole foot.

Sliding on the heel in a forwards direction while bending the left leg, then stepping on the right foot.

Gestures of the Arms

A gesture of the arm is written in the column for the arm. The whole arm moves from the shoulder joint and the direction and level is judged by the line in space between the shoulder joint and hand. The appropriate direction symbol is placed in the arm gesture column to indicate whether the arm is forwards, sideways or backwards of the shoulder joint.

Direction and Level

A *low level* arm gesture is below shoulder level, slanting downward.

Example:

116.

The right arm is forward and the left arm is backward at low level.

A *middle level* arm gesture is at shoulder level, horizontal.

Example:

117.

Both arms are sideways horizontal from the body, at middle level.

A *high level* arm gesture is above shoulder level, slanting upward.

Example:

118.

Both arms are held forward high.

Examples:

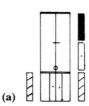

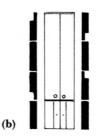

119. (a)   (b)

The arms start held high above the head (place high), the right arm moves in towards the shoulder (place middle), then is placed beside the body (place deep), whilst the left arm remains where it was.

The arms starting down move in opposition, passing by the sides of the body as they change direction.

Gestures of the Torso and Head

Movements of the head are written in the column to the right side of the vertical staff together with the pre sign for the head. Movements of the torso and parts of the torso (i.e. shoulder section, chest and pelvis) are written in the body columns on either side of the vertical staff together with the pre sign for that body part. The torso and pelvis are usually written in the left body column and the chest and shoulder section in the right body column.

Place high is the normal situation for the head, torso and parts of the torso.

Examples:

120. (a)   ℂ   (b)   ℂ

Use of columns for the specific body parts.

Normal position of the head, torso and parts of the torso.

Specific Action of Tilting

Direction and level are judged from the point of attachment of the body part to the new point in space of the extremity of that body part. The resulting directional change is a tilt or an inclination.

Examples:

121. (a) 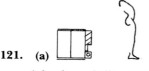   (b) 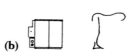   (c)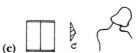

A backward tilt at high level of the chest.

A forward tilt at middle level of the torso.

A sideways inclination at high level of the head.

Cancellation of Gestures of the Body

The position of the arms, head, torso and parts of the torso in space is cancelled by the next directional indication. If there is a gap in the arm, head or body columns that body part retains its position in space.

Cancellation of Tilts

When you wish to return the torso or parts of the torso to their normal position after a tilting movement, the place high symbol may be used or the back to normal sign ⊙.

Examples:

 The torso tilts forward high and returns to place high, the normal standing position.

122.(a)

 The head tilts backwards high and returns to its normal position.

(b)

〈 and 〉 = a caret and means 'the same'. It is used to indicate movements of the same part of the body and avoids the repetition of the pre sign.

Specific Actions of Contraction and Extension

The contraction sign ✕ and the extension sign И are used to describe flexed and extended (narrow and wide) gestures.

When the limbs or torso use less space than normal, i.e., the limbs are drawn in towards the body and the torso shortens, the contraction sign can be used.

When the limbs or torso use more space than normal, i.e., the limbs extend away from the body and the torso stretches, the extension sign can be used.
The contraction sign or extension sign is placed before the direction symbol.

Contraction

Contraction is the drawing in of the extremity of a body part towards the place of attachment – in the case of the legs it is the hip joints and in that of the arms it is the shoulder joint.

Contraction of the Leg

Examples:

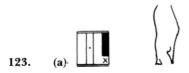

123. **(a)**

Slight shortening of the right leg when in the downward direction.

(b)

The left leg is pulled in more towards the hip whilst at sideways deep level (note the dotted line to indicate the side low direction).

Contraction of the Arm

Examples:

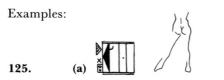

124. (a)

Slight shortening of the arms.

(b)

The right arm at middle level is pulled in more towards the body.

Contraction of the Torso

The contraction of the torso means a contraction over the front, side or back surfaces of the torso. It is a displacement of the centre part of the body whilst the base of the neck (free end) remains over the pelvis (fixed end). The head follows the curved line made by the spine.

Examples:

125. **(a)**

Slight contraction of the torso whilst inclining to the R side.

(b)

Double contraction of the torso whilst held in the normal position.

Extension

Extension is the lengthening of a part of the body into a particular direction.

Extension of the Legs

The normal state of the leg is that the knee, ankle and foot are relaxed but not bent. If you wish to indicate a straight leg the ⋈ sign is placed in front of the appropriate direction symbol.

Example:

126.

Standing on the right leg the left leg is extended in a straight line sideways deep.

Extension of the Arms

The arm is normally held with a relaxed, very slightly curved elbow and wrist. If you wish to indicate a straight arm, the ⋈ is placed below the appropriate direction symbol.

Example:

127.

The right arm is extended forwards deep in a straight line from the shoulder.

Extension of the Torso

The extension of a part of the body means that the body part stretches and a straight line in space is produced.

Examples:

128. **(a)** **(b)**

A stretching of the chest whilst held in the normal upright position.

A stretching of the torso whilst tilting forward producing a straight, flat back.

Specific Action of Bending

Bending of a body part is described as the moving of the free end of the body part over and away from the line of direction to join the fixed end of that body part.

A single joint action produces an angular shape, for instance, a bending of the elbow will result in a folding action of the arm.

A bending action of a multi-jointed part of the body, for instance, the torso, will produce a curving action and results in a curved shape.

The sign for bending (folding or curving) is ⩔ .

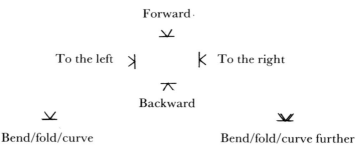

Forward

To the left ⟩ 〈 To the right

Backward

129. Bend/fold/curve   Bend/fold/curve further

Cancellation of Bending

The sign for the cancellation of a bend is ⩑ .

Examples:

130. **(a)**

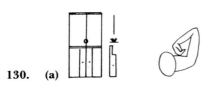

The folding of the right elbow produces an angular shape in the arm.

(b)

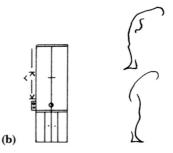

The torso bends forward then backwards, producing curved shapes.

(c)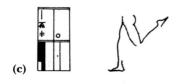

The knee fold results in a lift of the lower leg upwards.

(d)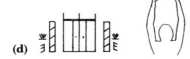

In the starting position the arms are held up high with the wrists bent in towards the centre of the body.

Specific Action of Circling

A circle made by a particular part of the body can be indicated by describing the points in space through which that part of the body passes.

Examples:

131. **(a)**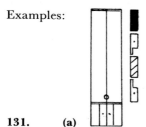

The right arm makes a circle travelling forward, up, back and down, ending by the side of the body. This circle lies in the sagittal plane.

(b)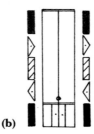

Both arms perform a lateral (sideways) circle, travelling left sideways, up above the shoulder to right sideways and finishing down by the sides of the body.

(c)

Standing on the left leg, the right leg at low level gestures forwards, then sideways, then backwards, ending by the side of the left leg, just off the ground, not carrying weight.

(d)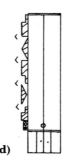

A clockwise circular pattern made by the torso, inclining first forward, then to the right, backward, to the left and ending forward.

PRACTICE IN READING AND WRITING

P. 28. Read and dance the following patterns:

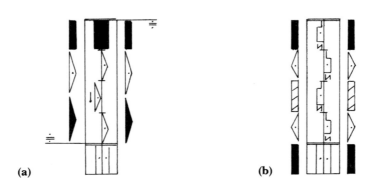

(a)　　　　　　　　　　　　(b)

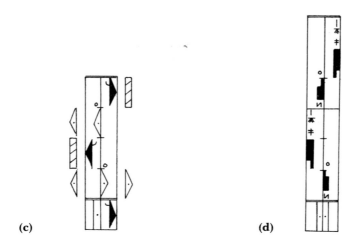

(c)　　　　　　　　　　　　(d)

P. 29. Choose an appropriate peice of music and develop the following patterns:

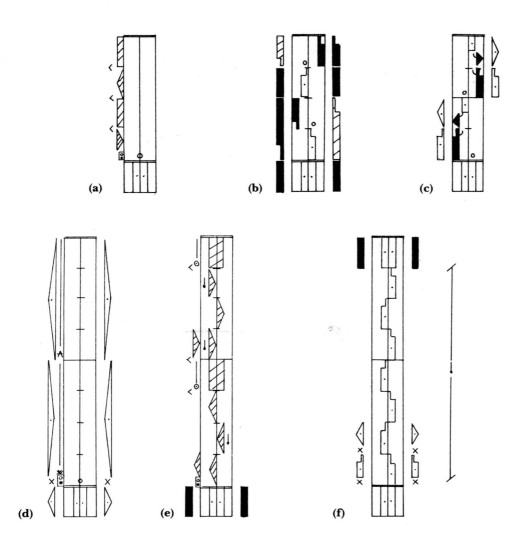

(a)   (b)   (c)

(d)   (e)   (f)

P. 30. (a) Compose and notate a sequence of body and arm circles.

(b) Compose and notate a series of step patterns which could be used in a dance about making a journey.

(c) Compose and notate a dance about freedom where the use of the body illustrates the struggle to be free.

(d) Compose and notate a dance involving two people, one a dominant character and the other a less strong character. Use contraction and extension of body shape as the starting points for your dance.

P. 31. Sequences from the ballet 'Echoi 11' choreographed by Jaap Flier.

Inner Subsidiary Column

The staff is often extended to include a second column for supporting, thus enabling you to indicate clearly that a dancer is supporting on more than one body part.

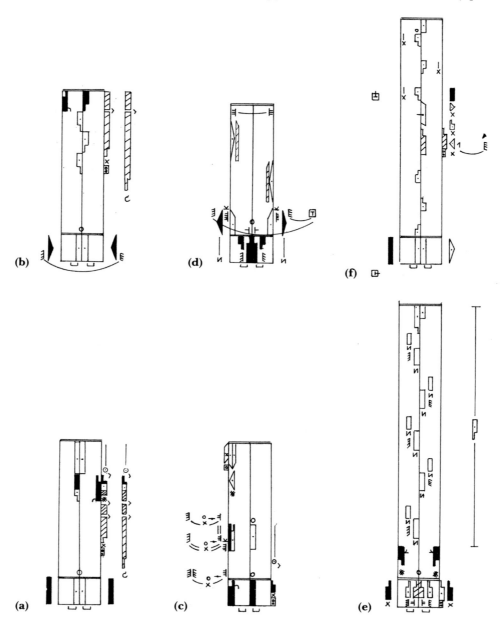

(a) (b) (c) (d) (e) (f)

Part 6
Jumping

A gap between symbols in the support column means that there is no support, the dancer is in the air. Jumping is, therefore, written by leaving a space in both support columns.

Example:

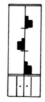

The dancer is in the air between forward steps, i.e., leaping.

132.

The amount of space left between support symbols indicates how long the dancer is in the air. Therefore, the longer the space in the support column the longer the time spent in the air – this will often produce longer or higher jumps.

Examples:

133.   **(a)** 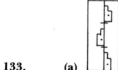   **(b)**   **(c)**

A moment spent in the air, i.e., short runs.

Half a beat spent in the air, i.e., leaps.

A lot of time spent in the air, i.e., high or long leaps.

The Five Basic Forms of Jumping

Examples:

134.   **(a)** 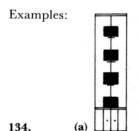   **(b)** 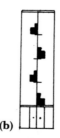   **(c)**

Jump: from both feet to both feet.

Leap: from one foot to the other.

Hop: from one foot to the same.

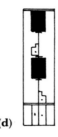

(d)

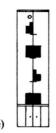

(e)

Assemblé: from one foot
to both feet.

Sissone: from both feet to
one foot.

Timing of Jumps

The landing from a jump may be sudden, i.e. the landing position is achieved quickly, or it may be sustained, i.e. the landing position takes longer.

Examples:

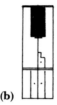

135.   **(a)**   **(b)**

Sudden landing   Sustained landing

On beat, Off beat Jumps

A different effect is produced by landing on or off the beat. Most forms of jump land on the beat. If a jump is to land on the beat, the moment in the air must come before the beat. If a jump is to land off the beat, the moment in the air must be on the beat.

Examples:

Preparation before the
count of 1

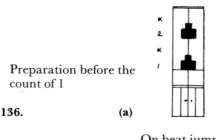

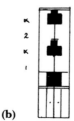

136.   **(a)**

(b)

On beat jumps   Off beat jumps

Examples:

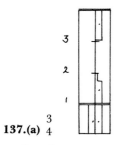

137.(a) $\frac{3}{4}$

Step hop involving a
whole beat in the air.

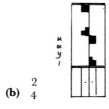

(b) $\frac{2}{4}$

A skip where the dancer
steps on count 1 and the
hop lands on the last part
of the beat.

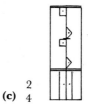

(c) $\frac{2}{4}$

A gallop where the
dancer is in the air on the
middle section of the
beat.

Jumps with Leg Gestures

Leg gestures may be used with all forms of jumps. The legs may extend, contract or
touch whilst in the air. The quality of the basic jump will change according to the
direction, level and timing of the leg gestures used.

Examples:

138. (a)

The legs move sidewards
in the air.

(b)

The legs contract under
the body during the
jump.

(c)

The left leg stretches and
gestures backwards.

(d)

The left leg gestures
forward during the
forward step hop.

(e)

The legs gesture at
middle level.

(f)

The legs touch in the air.

PRACTICE IN READING AND WRITING

P. 32. Read and dance the following patterns:

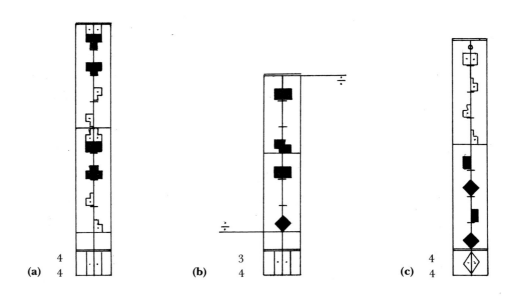

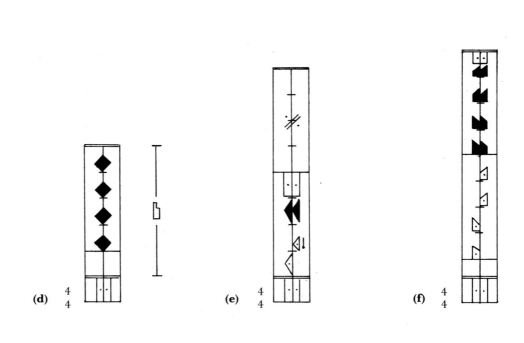

P. 33. Read and dance the following patterns. Select an appropriate piece of music and use the patterns as starting points for a dance.

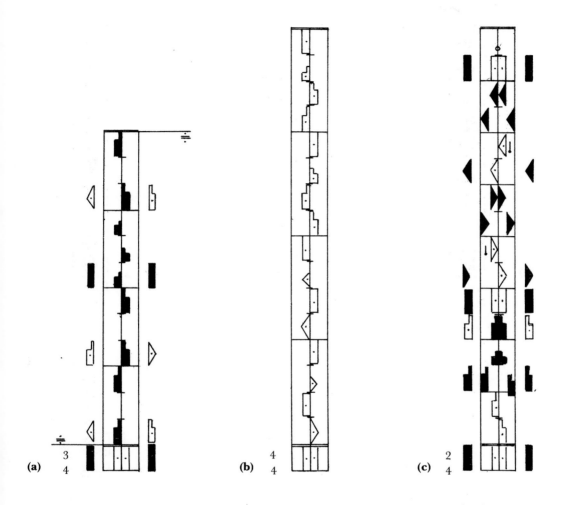

(a) 3/4 (b) 4/4 (c) 2/4

P. 34. (a) Compose and notate a circular pattern involving skips.
(b) Compose and notate a leaping pattern which travels from one side of the stage to the other.
(c) Compose and notate some jumping patterns which could be used in a dance about children's games.
(d) Compose and notate a hop scotch dance.

Part 7
Turning

Turns

The turn symbol is used for turns of the body as a whole and for rotations or twists of parts of the body.

The indication for a turn of the whole body is made by placing the turn sign in the support column.

The indication of the part of body that is to turn is made by placing the turn sign in the appropriate column of the vertical staff.

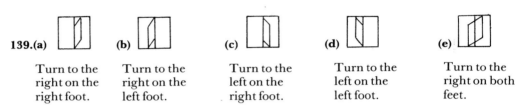

139.(a) Turn to the right on the right foot.

(b) Turn to the right on the left foot.

(c) Turn to the left on the right foot.

(d) Turn to the left on the left foot.

(e) Turn to the right on both feet.

Black pins are placed within the turn sign and indicate the amount of turn made (see page **15.**).

Examples:

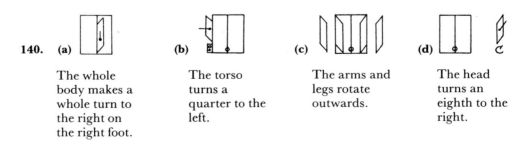

140. **(a)** The whole body makes a whole turn to the right on the right foot.

(b) The torso turns a quarter to the left.

(c) The arms and legs rotate outwards.

(d) The head turns an eighth to the right.

Steps and turns

A turn can happen before a step, after a step or during a step.

The turn before a step

A turn often occurs just before a step and is often a preparation for stepping into a new direction.

Example:

141.

A quarter turn to the right on the left foot, preparation for the step forwards on the right foot on the count of 1.

The step and turn at the same time

When the step and turn happen together, so that there is blending together of the two actions, the symbols are tied together with a vertical bow. This bow indicates that two different movements written one after the other should occur simultaneously.

142.   **(a)**

Simultaneous bow

(b)

The step and quarter turn happen at the same time.

Level of turns

A turn is performed at the same level as the previous step.

Examples:

143.   **(a)**

A quarter turn clockwise at middle level.

(b)

A half turn counterclockwise at low level.

(c)

A full turn clockwise at high level.

If there is a change of level during a turn, it can be shown by shading the turn sign. When a change of level occurs at the beginning of a turn, the beginning of the turn sign is shaded; when it occurs at the end, the end of the symbol is shaded; when it occurs throughout the movement the whole sign is shaded leaving enough space for the appropriate sign.

Examples:

144.   **(a)**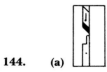

Sink at the beginning of the whole turn.

(b)

End the turn at middle level.

(c)

Rise throughout the whole turn.

Turning in the air

A turn in the air involves turning the whole body whilst it is unsupported.

To indicate a turn in the air, the turn sign is written across both support columns and action strokes or direction symbols are placed in the leg gesture columns to indicate that both legs are in the air.

Examples:

145. (a)

A whole turn in the air.

(b)

A half turn in the air, whilst legs gesture to the sides.

Front signs

We have seen in earlier sections the use of front signs to indicate which direction of the stage the dancer is facing. A front sign usually appears at the start of a score as part of the starting position and during a score the front sign is given after each turn. (see page **16**).

Example:

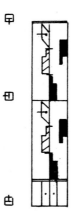

The front sign is written after each quarter turn.

146.

PRACTICE IN READING AND WRITING

P. 35. Read and dance the following patterns:

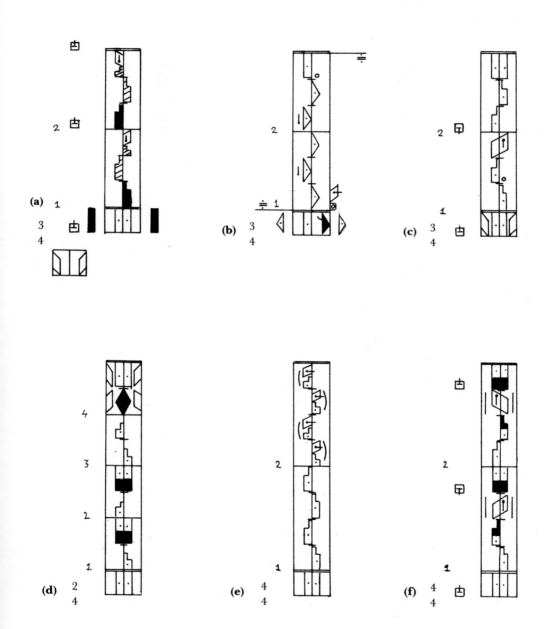

P. 36. Choose an appropriate piece of music and develop the following patterns:

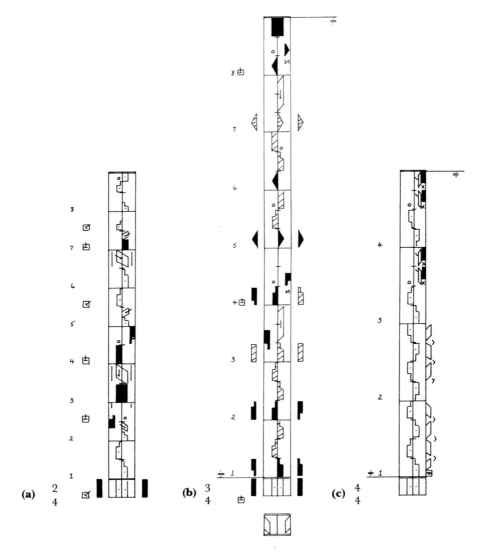

(a) $\frac{2}{4}$ **(b)** $\frac{3}{4}$ **(c)** $\frac{4}{4}$

Notate the following:

P. 37. (a) Compose a travelling pattern which involves sudden and sustained turns.

(b) Compose and notate a turning and jumping sequence which travels diagonally across the stage.

(c) Compose and notate a turning sequence for two dancers.

(d) Using different types of turns, compose and notate a motif for a dance about joy, fear or anger.

(e) Compose and notate a group dance where the initial relationship is one of hostility which resolves into friendship.

P. 38. The detailed score of the extract from the ballet 'Echoi II' by Jaap Flier.

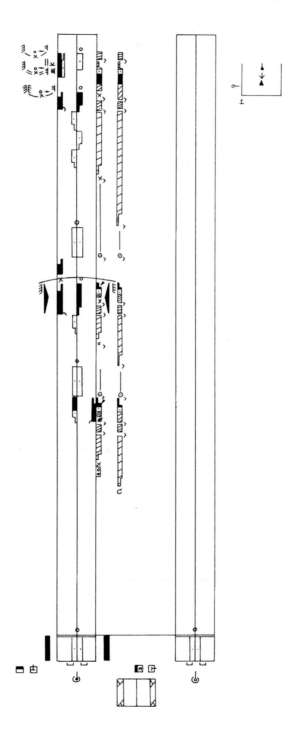

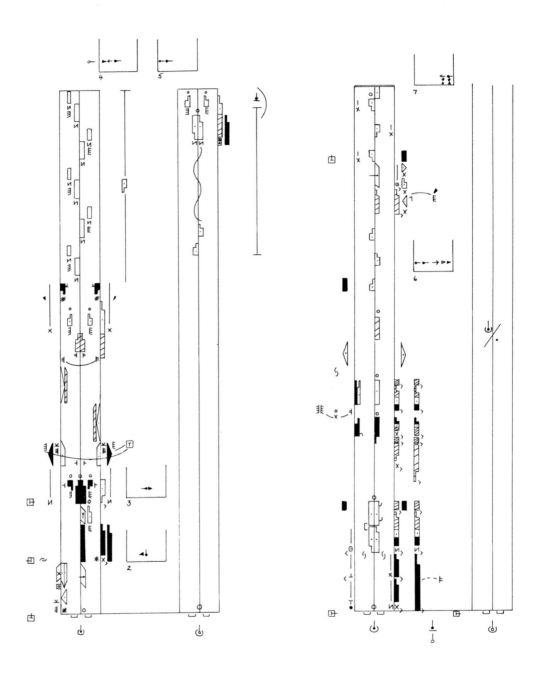

Benesh Movement Notation

Acknowledgments

Notation examples by Linda Pilkington F.I.Chor., F.I.S.T.D., and Enrico Cecchetti Diploma A.I.S.T.D.

My thanks to the Staff and Colleagues of the Institute of Choreology for their assistance in the compilation of this section.

The following extracts are quoted with the kind permission of the Score Owners and Choreographers, where appropriate. Choreography copyright is established when the work is recorded. Where relevant, the date of the score and the place where the work was notated are given.

TITLE	CHOREOGRAPHER	SCORE OWNER
"The Rite of Spring"	Richard Alston © London 1981	Mercury Theatre Trust Ltd.
"Ghost Dances"	Christopher Bruce © London 1981	Mercury Theatre Trust Ltd.
"Dances of Love and Death"	Robert Cohan © London 1981	Institute of Choreology
"Something to Tell"	Siobhan Davies © London 1980	Institute of Choreology
"Las Hermanas"	Kenneth MacMillan © Stuttgart 1963	Royal Opera House
"The Rite of Spring"	Kenneth MacMillan © London 1962	Royal Opera House
"Voluntaries"	Glen Tetley © London 1976	Royal Opera House
"4 Schumann Pieces"	Hans van Manen © London 1975	Royal Opera House
"Swan Lake" Act II	Lev Ivanov	Institute of Choreology
"La Bayadére"	Marius Petipa	Institute of Choreology

Introduction

Benesh Movement Notation was invented in England by Joan and Rudolf Benesh in the late 1940's.

Joan Benesh (née Rothwell) was a dancer in the Sadler's Wells Ballet. Her interest in choreography was the starting point of the collaboration which was to last until her husband's death in 1975.

Rudolf Benesh's first profession was Accountancy. His gifts as a musician and artist were to complement his mathematical knowledge in the development of a system of movement notation.

The system was publicly launched in 1955. Its use was adopted by The Royal Ballet and leading dance schools. Applications to other movement fields soon followed. In 1962, the Beneshes founded the Institute of Choreology to co-ordinate development.

Rudolf Benesh defined Choreology as the scientific and aesthetic study of all forms of human movement through movement notation.

Structure

Benesh Movement Notation is written from left to right on a five-line stave.

Floor patterns are written *below* the stave.

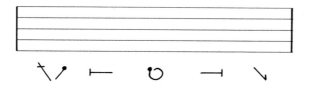

Direction, Location and Travel for the Solo Dancer and Groups are described in Part I.

Limb and Body Movements are plotted *in* the stave.

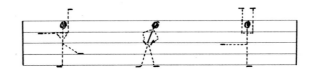

This illustration shows how the dancer 'fits' into the stave. You will study a method which is both more economic and comprehensive than these stick figures.

The usage of signs which represent the hands, elbows, feet, knees, head and body parts is described in Part II.

Rhythm and Phrasing are shown *above* the stave.

This information is described in Part III.

Parts I, II and III are concerned with different elements of composition. Each of these Parts is designed to be studied independently.

Part IV – Linking Information – combines below-stave, in-stave *and* above-stave information. It illustrates usage of the full structure of the system. Jumping, stepping, sliding, and repeated patterns of movement are introduced in this Part.

Extracts from Choreographic works are quoted in Parts I and IV. They are identified as follows: "Title" – Choreographer/Composer.

Each Part includes tasks which explore the theoretical and practical understanding of the material. These exercises are written in *italics*.

Part I

Below-stave information

Direction.

The sign to show the direction a dancer faces is a "pin" ⏐ . Think of this pin as an arrow, ↑ , the head of the arrow being represented by the head of the pin.

The direction in which the head of the pin (the arrowhead) points is the direction faced.

If the pin points to the top of the page, the dancer is facing the *Front* of the performing area.

If the pin points to the bottom of the page, the dancer is facing the *Back* of the performing area.

And so on.

Summary

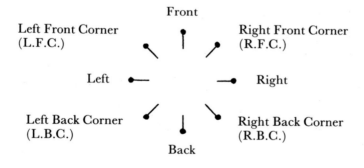

Prone

When you lie on your stomach, you are in the horizontal position called Prone.

Face Front ⏐ – think of falling forwards onto the floor. Add a short line in front of the head of the direction sign. ⏐

Supine

When you lie on your back, you are in the horizontal position called Supine.

Face Front ⥮ – think of falling backwards onto the floor. Add a short line behind the head of the direction sign. ⥮

Summary

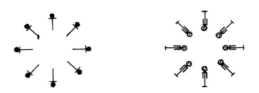

On your side

Right Side: Face Front ⥮ – think of falling to your right. ⥮
Left Side: Face Front ⥮ – think of falling to your left. ⥮

Summary – on your *right* side   Summary – on your *left* side

Changing Direction

When changing direction, 'Take the shortest route' is the rule.
e.g. Turn from Front ⥮ to face Right ⟶•

A right turn = 90°, a turn to the left = 270°, therefore turn to your right.

Face the following directions:

1. ⟶•   2. ↓   3. •⟶   4. ⟋   5. ⟍   6. ⥮

When the route offers a choice such as turning from (a) •⟶ to (b)⟶•, more information is required.

Show the route by curving the tail of the direction sign.

Start facing Front. Turn towards your right shoulder to face Back.

You have made a half turn to the right.

Start facing Right. Turn towards your right shoulder to face Left.

Another half turn to the right.

For turns of less than half a circle, it is not essential to draw a curved tail. This is because the shortest route rule applies. However the curved tail gives a more immediate picture of the turn.

Start facing L.F.C. and turn to face Right.

↖   *Either* show the new direction   ⟶   *or* 'draw' the turn ↻ .

Examples of Turning Signs.

a. ↻   b. ↻   c. ↝   d. ↷   e. ↻

$\frac{1}{8}$ $\frac{1}{4}$ $\frac{3}{8}$ $\frac{1}{2}$ $\frac{5}{8}$

f. ↺   g. ↺   h. ↺   i. ②

$\frac{3}{4}$ $\frac{7}{8}$ Full turn   two full turns

Note that the number of turns is written inside the turning sign.

Copy out turning signs (a) to (i) above.
Now write them turning 'to the other side' – this means instead of turning to the right turn to the left.

Describe the following turns:
e.g. ↺ *Start facing R.F.C., turn to the right and finish facing Left.*

a. ↻   b. ↺

c. ↺   d. ↻

e. ∪   f. ↻

g. ②   h. ②

The next examples are alternating turns which may be performed in sequence.

Write these turns 'to the other side' and describe your answers.

1. ↝   2. ↻   3. ↝

4. ↻   5. ↷   6. ↻

7. ↻   8. ↻   9. ②

Location

Location is the term used to describe the whereabouts of a dancer in a performing area.

The diagram below represents the performing area. This diagram is referred to as an Area Matrix or Stage Plan.

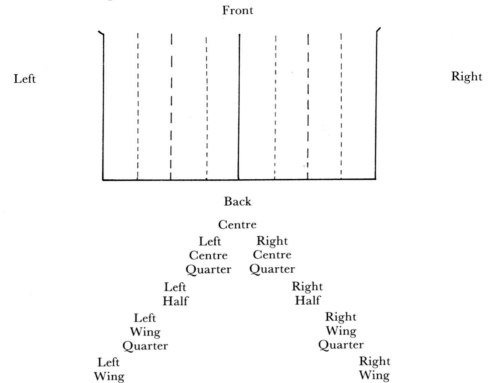

The nine vertical divisions are represented by Location Signs.

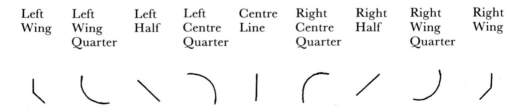

Practise drawing location signs:
Be sure the signs representing the left side of the stage relate to a left diagonal and vice versa e.g.

The dancer's position on stage is shown by drawing a small horizontal dash through the relevant location sign.

Examples on the Centre Line.

a. ⊤ Dancer in Centre Front.

b. ⊤ Dancer is midway between Centre Front and Centre Stage.

c. † Dancer is Centre Stage.

d. ⊥ Dancer is midway between Centre Stage and Centre back.

e. ⊥ Dancer is Centre Back.

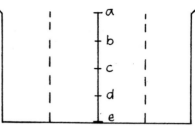

Examples – Stage Left and Stage Right

f. � Dancer is at the Front of the Left Wing Quarter

g. ⊼ Dancer is midway between the Front and the Middle of the Left Half

h. ⊁ Dancer is on the Middle of the Left Centre Quarter

i. ƒ Dancer is midway between the Middle and the Back of the Right Centre Quarter

j. ⊬ Dancer is on the Middle of the Right Half

k. ⊐ Dancer is midway between the Front and the Middle of the Right Wing Quarter

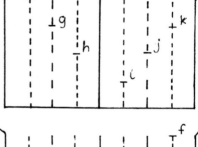

Notate the locations marked on this stage plan:

Note that they are the 'opposite' locations to those shown on the previous plan i.e. Right and Left are reversed.

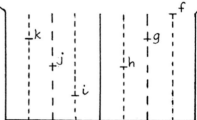

Draw a horizontal dash to the right or left of a location sign to show the dancer's corresponding position on stage.

l. ⊏ To the right of the Left Wing

m. ⊰ To the left of the Left Wing Quarter

n. ⊼ To the right of the Left Half

o. ⊐ To the left of the Left Centre Quarter

p. ⌊ To the right of the Centre Back

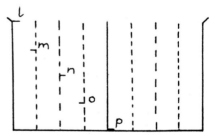

Notate the 'opposite' locations as marked on this stage plan:

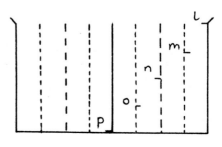

Use of Location and Direction

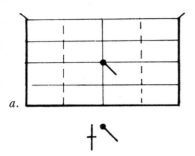

a.

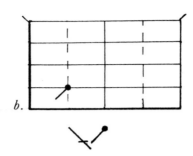

b.

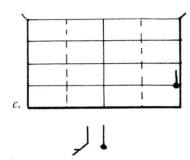

c.

See how the location and direction shown on Stage Plans(a) – (c) are notated.
Note that the *head* of the direction sign represents the exact whereabouts of the dancer.

Location is written *before* Direction.

Show the whereabouts of the dancer on stage plans (d) – (i):-

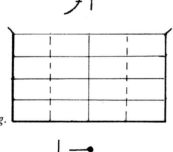

d.

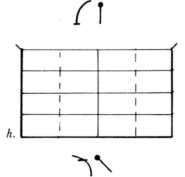

e.

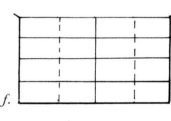

f.

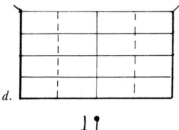

g.

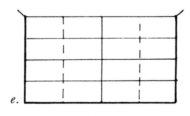

h.

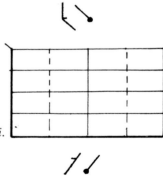

i.

Notate stage plans (j) – (o):

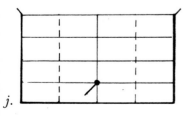

j.

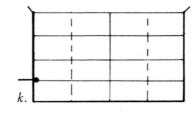

k.

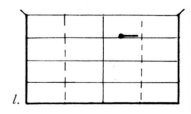

l.

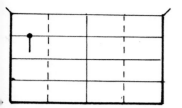 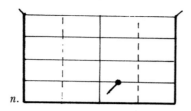 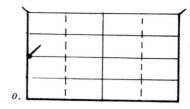

Travelling – Straight Paths

An arrow points in a certain direction.

⟶ This arrow points to the right. Travel towards the *Right* of the stage.

This arrow shows you your *path* of travel but *how* do you travel? Forwards? Sideways?

By adapting an arrow, the answer is provided.

arrowhead

feathers (think of a dart).

Split the arrow into four –

Each of these parts of the arrow shows the same path of travel. They are pointing to the top of the page and therefore you are travelling toward the Front of the stage.

When travelling *forwards*, think of your right shoulder.

> The right part of the arrowhead represents your right shoulder.
> You are travelling *forwards*, towards the Front.

When travelling *backwards*, again think of your *right* shoulder.

> The left part of the arrowhead also represents your *right* shoulder but it is on the left of the path of travel.
> You are travelling *backwards*, towards the Front.

When travelling *sideways*, think of your own front – your chest or stomach.

> This feather represents your own front which is facing the Right side of the stage.
> The arrow is still pointing towards the top of the page.
> You are travelling *sideways*, to your left, towards the Front.

> Your front is now facing the Left side of the stage.
> You are travelling *sideways*, to your right, towards the Front.

In the diagrams below, each travelling sign is shown in relation to the direction at the centre.

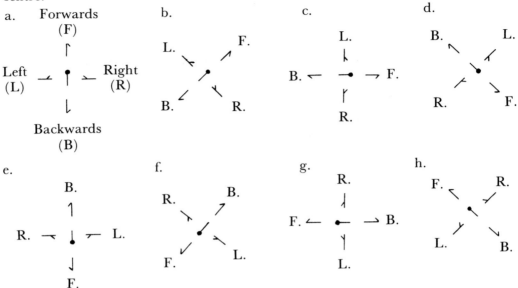

Copy out each of the travelling signs in diagrams (a) – (h). Write the signs in the following order – Forwards, Right, Backwards, Left e.g. (a)

Perform each instruction.

Describe the following sequence:

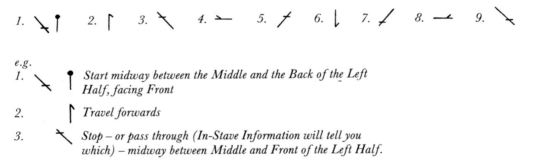

e.g.
1. Start midway between the Middle and the Back of the Left Half, facing Front

2. Travel forwards

3. Stop – or pass through (In-Stave Information will tell you which) – midway between Middle and Front of the Left Half.

Notate an example of a square floor pattern which includes changes of direction.
e.g. Face the direction of your square:

All the changes of direction in this sequence are quarter turns to the right. The 'shortest route' rule therefore applies. Remember that travelling signs incorporate directions.

Notate a square floor pattern which includes various changes in direction:

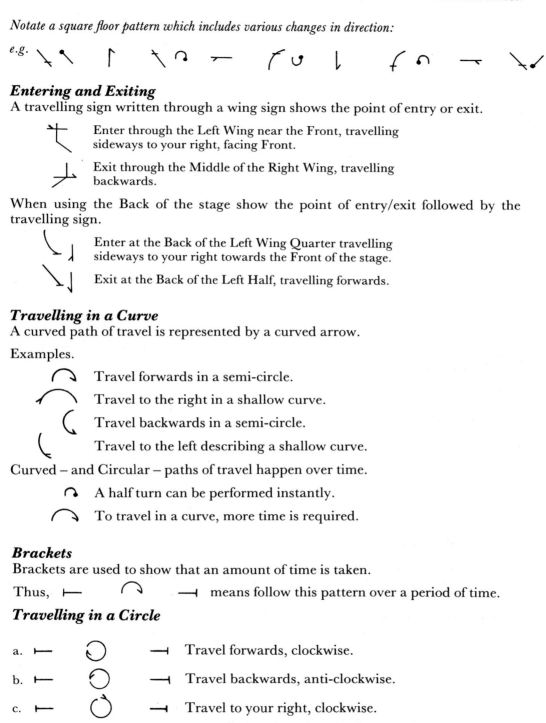

e.g.

Entering and Exiting

A travelling sign written through a wing sign shows the point of entry or exit.

Enter through the Left Wing near the Front, travelling sideways to your right, facing Front.

Exit through the Middle of the Right Wing, travelling backwards.

When using the Back of the stage show the point of entry/exit followed by the travelling sign.

Enter at the Back of the Left Wing Quarter travelling sideways to your right towards the Front of the stage.

Exit at the Back of the Left Half, travelling forwards.

Travelling in a Curve

A curved path of travel is represented by a curved arrow.

Examples.

Travel forwards in a semi-circle.

Travel to the right in a shallow curve.

Travel backwards in a semi-circle.

Travel to the left describing a shallow curve.

Curved – and Circular – paths of travel happen over time.

A half turn can be performed instantly.

To travel in a curve, more time is required.

Brackets

Brackets are used to show that an amount of time is taken.

Thus, ⊢   ⌒   ⊣ means follow this pattern over a period of time.

Travelling in a Circle

a. ⊢   ◯   ⊣   Travel forwards, clockwise.

b. ⊢   ◯   ⊣   Travel backwards, anti-clockwise.

c. ⊢   ◯   ⊣   Travel to your right, clockwise.

d. ⊢   ◯   ⊣   Travel to your left, anti-clockwise.

Note that in (c) and (d), you have your back to the centre of the circle.

e. ⊢—   ◯   —⊣   Travel to your left, clockwise.

f. ⊢—   ◯   —⊣   Travel to your right, anti-clockwise.

Note that in (e) and (f), you face the centre of the circle.

Show the size of your circle by recording its diameter. Draw two dashes on one location sign.

⊢—   ↕ ◯   —⊣   is a large circle, the diameter being almost the depth of the stage.

⊢—   ⤡ ◯   —⊣   is a small circle, near the Front of the Left Half.

Explore Curved and Circular Paths of Travel.

e.g.: a figure of eight

⟍⟋ ⊢— ⤿ ✝ ⌣ ⤴ ⌢ ✝ ⌣ ⟍ —⊣

This may be shown in a short form.

⟍⟋ ⊢— ⋁ ⨏ —⊣

Note that it is then necessary to notate only two locations.

Travelling – Rolling
Starting and finishing prone.

Start ⊺   Roll to the right ⤞—
You must turn to your left ↻
Combined sign ⤞⟲

The travelling sign incorporates the floor line.

Start ⊺   Roll to the left —⤝
You must turn to your right ↺
Combined sign ⟳⤝

Starting and finishing supine.

⟊ A roll to the right, while turning right ↷
⟊ A roll to the left, while turning left ↶

Starting and finishing on your right side.

⟊ A roll forwards, while turning to the right ↻
⟊ A roll backwards, while turning to the left ↺

Starting and finishing on your left side.

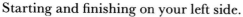 A roll forwards, while turning to your left

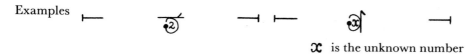 A roll backwards, while turning to your right

a. Start   *Notate a roll to the right.*

b. Start   *Notate a roll to the left.*

c. Start   *Notate a roll forwards.*

d. Start   *Notate a roll backwards.*

Multiple Rolls

As with upright turns, the number is written inside the turn sign.

Examples

$\mathcal{X}$ is the unknown number

Half Rolls

To the right

Starting   passing through   and finishing

To the left

Starting   passing through   and finishing

Forwards

Starting   passing through   and finishing

Backwards

Starting   passing through   and finishing

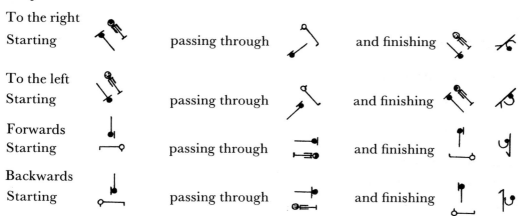

Notate three static horizontal direction signs for each of the following:

a.   *b.*

c.   *d.*

add the stick figures to check your answers.

e.g.

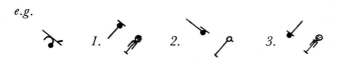 *1.*   *2.*   *3.*

SUMMARY – BELOW-STAVE INFORMATION – SOLO DANCER

Draw stage plans of the following sequence:

1. *Enter through the Left Wing near the Front of the stage, travelling backwards.*
2. *Stop on Left Half (still facing Left Wing).*
3. *Turn to the right to face Right Back Corner.*
4. *Start to travel forward.*
5. *Stop just to the right of the Right Wing Quarter near the Back of the stage. Face the Back.*
6. *Travel in a curve, sideways to your right.*
7. *Stop in the Middle of the Left Centre Quarter, facing the Left Wing.*
8. *Travel forwards. Exit through the Middle of the Right Wing.*

e.g. 1.

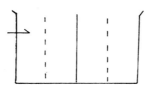

Notate the same sequence using below stave information.   e.g. ✝

Notate the floor patterns of a dance study which you have composed.
Show your starting position e.g. ＼ ✓

Include paths of travel e.g. ⊢— 〔 —⊣

and turns e.g. ｜ ）

Direction, Location and Travel – Groups

When showing groups, there are three points to be considered:

1. the direction faced by the dancers
2. the pattern
3. the number of dancers

Static Lines and Files

(a) ↑ ↑ ↑ ↑ ↑ ↑ – a *line* of 6 is summarised to ┼6

  The direction sign ↑ shows the direction faced.
  The line across the direction sign gives a 'picture' of the pattern.
  The number 6 denotes the number of dancers in the pattern. The dancers are equally spaced.

(b) —• —• —•   –a *file* of 3 is summarised to —•3

Here the sign —• shows the direction faced *and* gives a 'picture' of the pattern. This sign representing a file is larger than a direction sign representing an individual. The number 3 denotes the number of equally-spaced dancers.

Notate groups in the same order as you would describe them in words e.g. a line of six, a file of three.

When a pattern line is added to the direction sign, as in example (a), the formation is called a *line*.

When the pattern is incorporated in the direction sign, as in example (b), the formation is called a *file*.

Note the effect of direction on a formation.

In each of these patterns, the dancers have not moved from the spot.

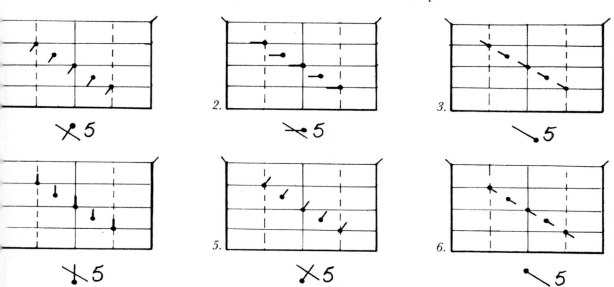

Location of Lines and Files

To summarise the location, or whereabouts on the stage, of a line or file, two locations signs are joined and the pattern added.

Location of the ends of the line/file   Summarised location

Order of information – Summarised Location, followed by Pattern, followed by Number of Dancers.

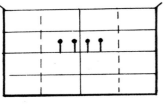 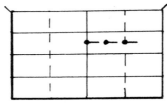

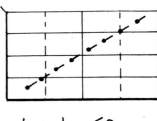 

When only one location sign is used, two small dashes give the length of the line/file.

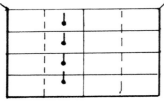 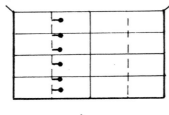

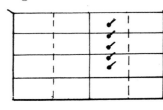

When the pattern line is too acute to be drawn easily on the location signs, either use two dashes to show the ends of the line/file or separate the location signs slightly.

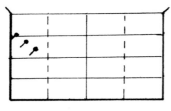 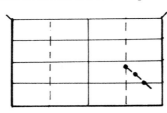 

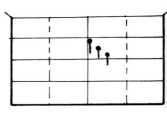 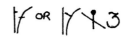

Copy out and complete the following:

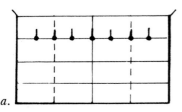 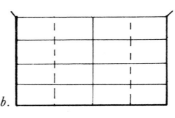 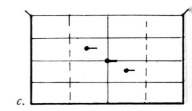

a. b. c.

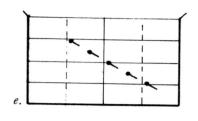

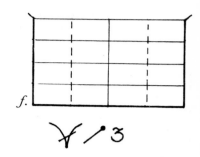

Travelling Lines and Files

⌐ ⌐ ⌐ ⌐ is summarised to —┼ 4

Path of travel and direction faced are shown by the travelling sign; the pattern line is added, and the number of dancers in the pattern is 4.

⌐— ⌐— ⌐— is summarised to ⌐—— 3

Path of travel and direction faced are shown by the travelling sign; the pattern line is incorporated in the sign, and the number of dancers in the pattern is 3.

Note that in travelling groups, the pattern line must be apparent. It is either incorporated in the travelling sign – see examples (a), (b) and (c) below – or drawn through the path of travel – see examples (d), (e) and (f).

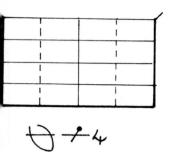

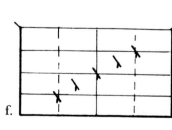

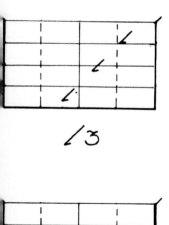

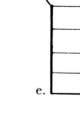

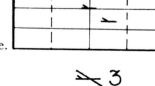

Entering and Exiting

When dancers enter or exit *one after the other*, a travelling sign written through a wing sign shows the point of entry or exit.

Eight dancers enter *one after the other* through the Left Wing near the Front.

Six dancers exit *one after the other* through the Middle of the Right Wing.

When dancers enter or exit *at the same time*, small dashes must be added to a wing sign to show the size of the formation.

Three dancers enter *at the same time* through the Right Wing, equally spaced from near the Front to near the Back i.e. widely spaced. Note the pattern line drawn through the travelling sign. The pattern line will always appear on the 'on-stage' side of the wing for entrances.

Here the dancers exit close together. The pattern line will always appear on the 'off-stage' side of the wing for exits.

Four dancers enter *at the same time* between the Middle and near the Back of the Left Wing.

Four dancers exit *at the same time* between near the Front and the Middle of the Right Wing.

When using the Back of the stage, show the point, or area of entry/exit followed by the travelling sign.

Three dancers enter *one after the other* through the Centre at the Back of the stage.

Four dancers exit *one after the other* through the Right Half at the Back of the stage.

Four dancers enter *at the same time* between the Centre and the Right Half at the Back of the stage.

Three dancers exit *at the same time* between the Left Wing Quarter and the Left Centre Quarter at the Back of the stage.

Copy out and complete the following:

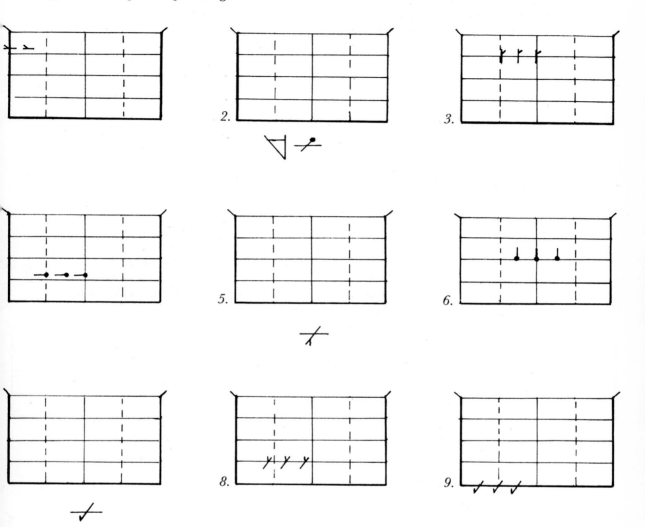

When writing in sequence, it is not necessary to repeat the number of dancers involved if there is no change from the previously stated information. Therefore, show the number of dancers in this sequence only below stage plan 1.

Curved Lines

There are two types of Curved Lines – radiating and non-radiating.

A radiating curve.

becomes ⋏5 The direction sign is written *through* the curve.

A non-radiating curve.

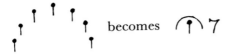 becomes

The direction sign and pattern line are written *separately*.

Curved Files

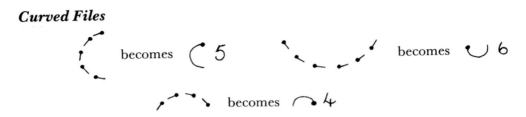

Locations for Curved Lines and Files.

Method 1. Attach the curve to the location signs.

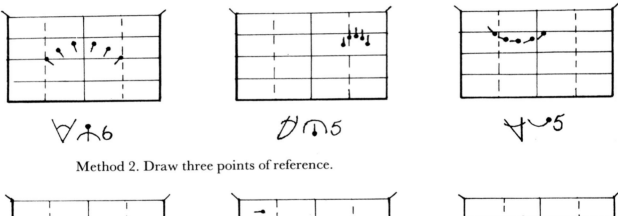

Method 2. Draw three points of reference.

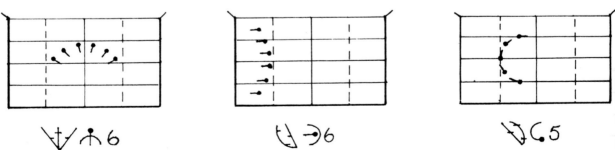

Method 1. gives a 'picture' of the curve.
Method 2. gives more specific information because it also locates the depth of the curve.

Copy out and complete the following:

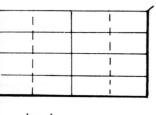

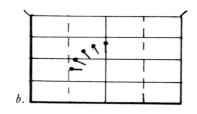
b.

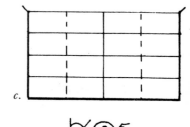
c.

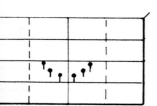

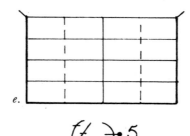
e.

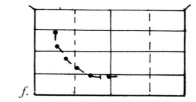
f.

Travelling Curves

Just as there are three types of curves –

I.   Radiating Curves

II.   Non-radiating Curves

III. Curved Files

– it follows that Curves can travel in three different ways:

I. Radiating Curves can become larger:

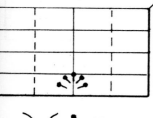

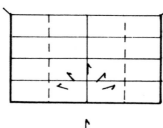

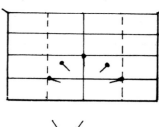

or smaller:

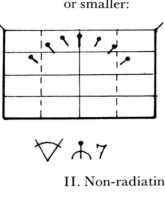
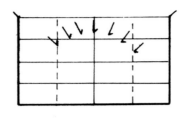
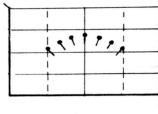

II. Non-radiating Curves will stay the same size but travel to a different location:

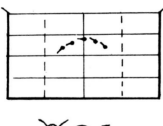
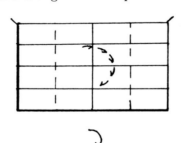
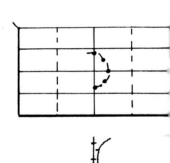

III. Curved Files will travel along their own pattern:

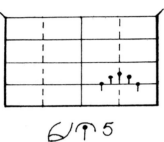
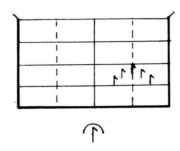
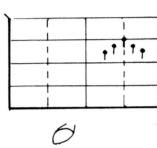

In the following sequence, note the use of numbers to show who is moving.

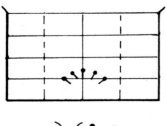
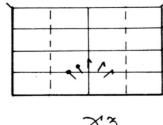
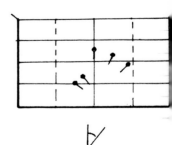

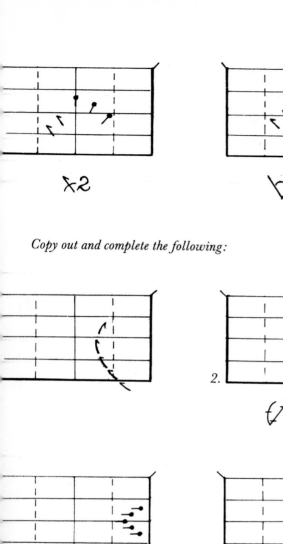

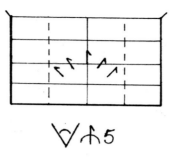

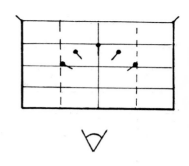

Copy out and complete the following:

2.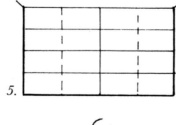

3.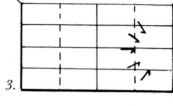

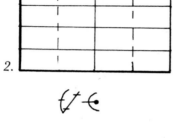

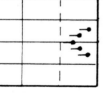

5.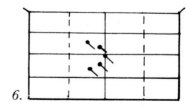

6.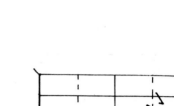

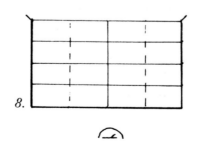

8.

9.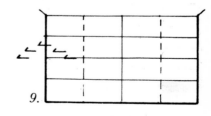

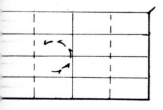

Circles
Radiating Circles

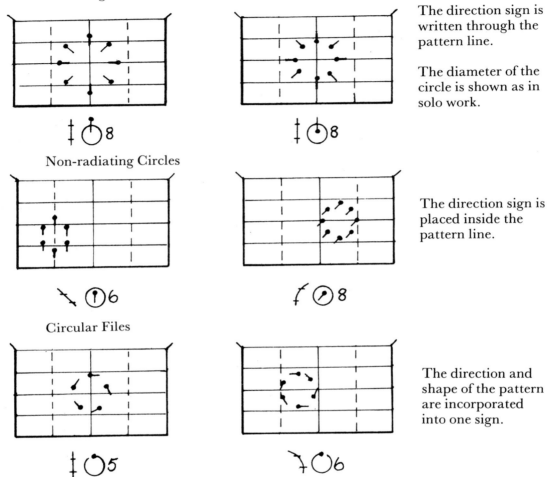

The direction sign is written through the pattern line.

The diameter of the circle is shown as in solo work.

Non-radiating Circles

The direction sign is placed inside the pattern line.

Circular Files

The direction and shape of the pattern are incorporated into one sign.

It is important to note if there is a dancer at the *centre front* of a circle or if there is no-one centre front.

Compare

a. Dancer at centre front.

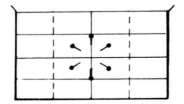

with b. No-one centre front.

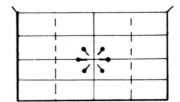

Both are Radiating Circles made up of 6 dancers.

a. 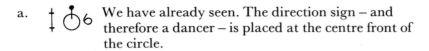 We have already seen. The direction sign – and therefore a dancer – is placed at the centre front of the circle.

b. 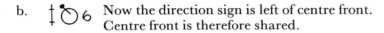 Now the direction sign is left of centre front. Centre front is therefore shared.

In Non-radiating Circles, a small dash on the pattern line to the left of centre front tells you that the centre front of the circle is shared.

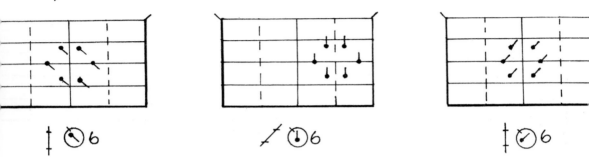

When centre front is shared in Circular Files, draw the dancer to the left of centre front.

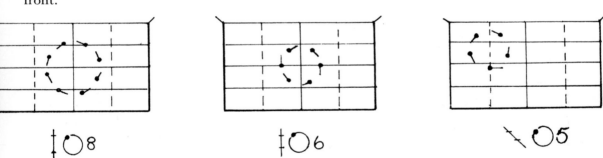

Travelling Circles

As with Curves, Circles can move in three ways.

I. They can become smaller or larger:

Smaller   Larger

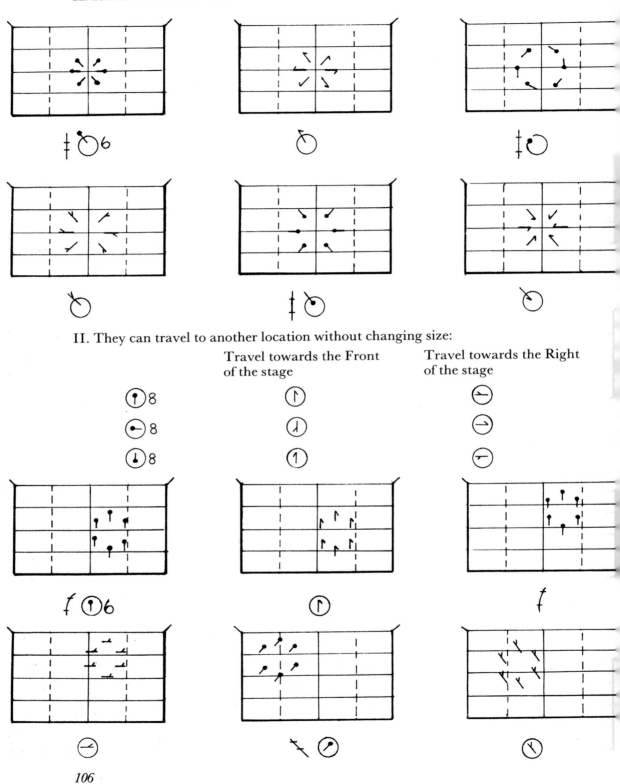

II. They can travel to another location without changing size:

Travel towards the Front of the stage

Travel towards the Right of the stage

III. They can revolve:

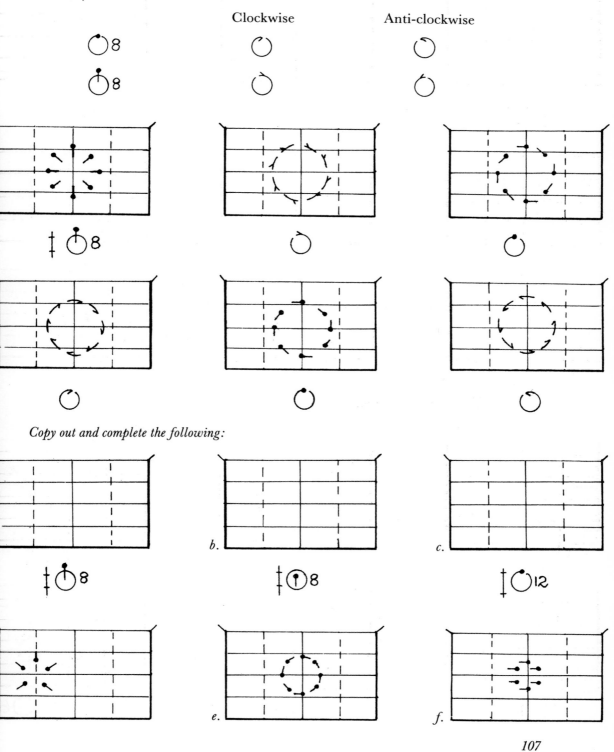

Copy out and complete the following:

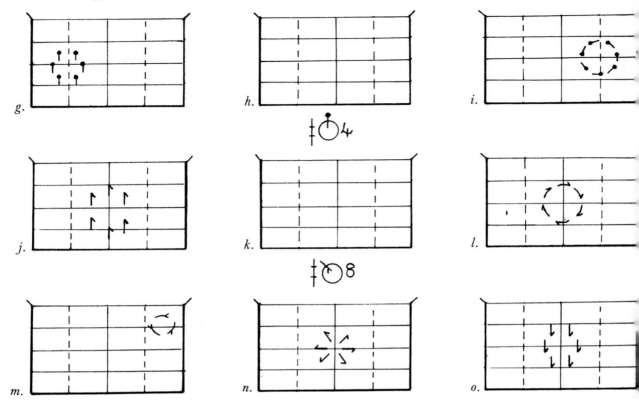

Multiple Patterns

You may wish to use combinations of lines, files, curves and circles.

Examples.

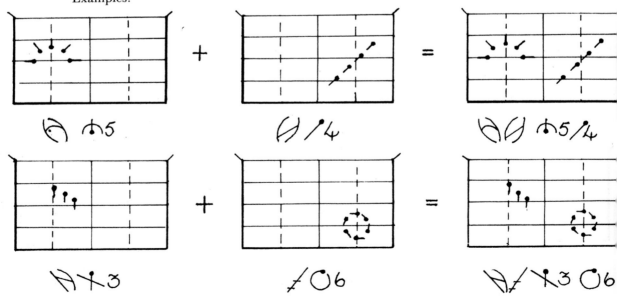

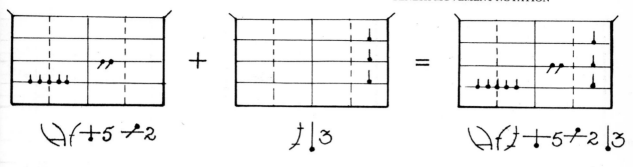

Reflected Patterns

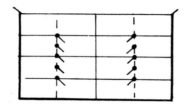

In this Stage Plan, the pattern on the right side of the stage is a mirror image of the pattern on the left side of the stage.

Notate only the *left* side of the stage and use the reflection sign // to show that the pattern and movement are reflected onto the right side.

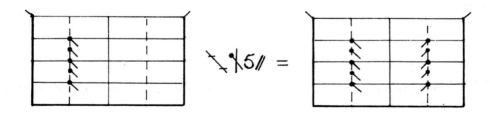

Examples:

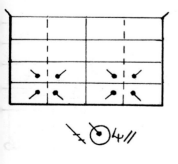

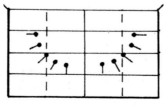

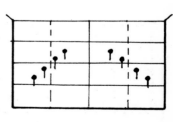

Compose a dance study using the following stage patterns:

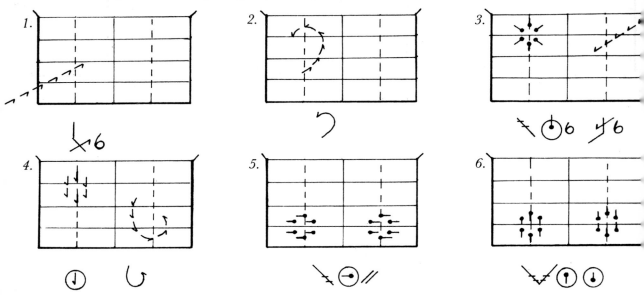

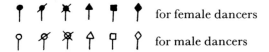

Reminder – Note that when writing in sequence it is not necessary to repeat the number of dancers involved if there is no change from the previously stated information.

Identification Signs

So far this Part has been dealing with dancers in what might be called 'formal' groups. We have learnt to read and record in summarised form Lines, Files, Curves, Circles and Multiple and Reflected Patterns.

Often an important concern is to keep track of individuals; we must give each dancer or character an identity which we can follow throughout the score.

     for female dancers

     for male dancers

Any symbol may be assigned to a particular dancer. But choose carefully. Each symbol should be easy to write and easy to recognise.

Stage Plans give an immediate picture of relationships.

Follow the progress of ⃒Ann, ⃒ Jenny and ⃒ Marie.

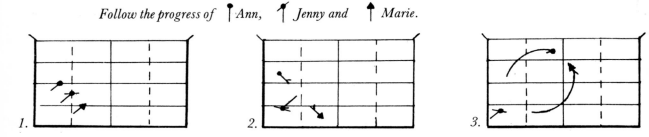

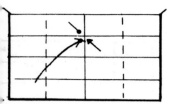 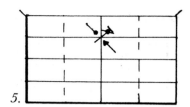 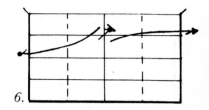

5. 6.

Extract – 'Something to Tell' – Davies/Britten

A plan of the set

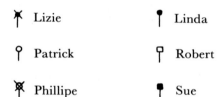

— Bench

♦ Chair

〰 Venetian Blind

Cast List:

Lizie   Linda

Patrick   Robert

Phillipe   Sue

Now you can identify and follow the paths of travel of each dancer.

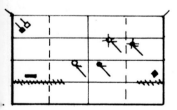 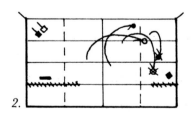 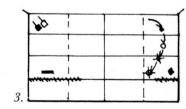

2. 3.

SUMMARY – BELOW-STAVE INFORMATION – GROUPS

We have now dealt with two methods of recording Static and Travelling Groups. The first method presents the information in a precise and economic form.

Example – Extract from Act II of 'Swan Lake' – Ivanov/Tchaikowsky

Draw the stage plans of the asterisked formations identifying the position of two particular Swans ✶ *and* ↟ *who start as shown in the opening formation.*

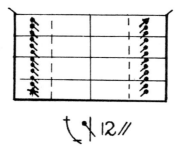

The second method is the drawing within stage plans of identified individuals. These give an immediate picture of the relationships of the individuals.

Extract – 'Las Hermanas' 1st movement – MacMillan/Martin

Cast List

↑ Marcia – Eldest Sister   ✶ Ruth – Mother

↟ Birgit – Youngest Sister   ✦ Helga – Jealous Sister

↑ Gisela
↟ Edith
} – Middle Sisters

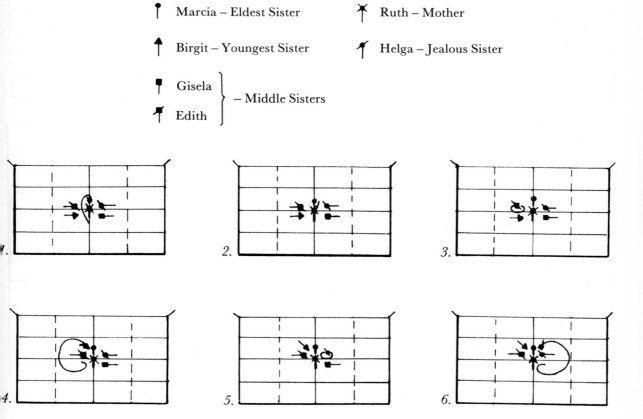

(i) *Who is moving in stage plan 1?*
(ii) *Identify the dancer and describe her movement in stage plans 3, 4, 5 and 6.*
(iii) *Write the names of the dancers where they finish in stage plan 6.*

Example: Stage Plan 1.

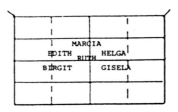

Compose a study for two or more dancers.

Choose a theme such as 'overtaking' each other, or 'dodging each other'.

Draw a stage plan for each manoeuvre.

e.g. ↑ *Sally* ↓ *Bill*

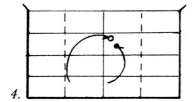

1.

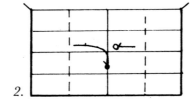

2.

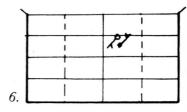

3.

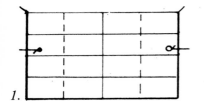

4.

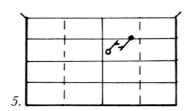

5.

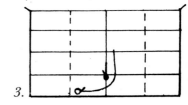

6.

Part II
In-stave information

Body Matrix

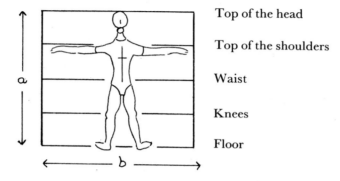

Top of the head

Top of the shoulders

Waist

Knees

Floor

The Body Matrix is a 'square' frame.

Side (b) of the body matrix is longer than side (a). This is to counteract the visual illusion which causes (a) to appear longer than (b) in a perfectly drawn square.

Therefore each frame is a visual square and not an actual square.

Always notate as if you are behind the dancer. You can then easily identify movement in the same way as the dancer does. Right is right and left is left.

Level Sign

— A horizontal stroke represents a hand or foot which is *level* with the body.

Imagine that you are facing a wall in the position shown above. By marking the location of your hands and feet on the wall, you will automatically fix the placing of your limbs.

 In this position, your hands and feet are level.

The dotted line drawn through the centre of the frame is not part of the Notation. It is used here as a guide for drawing the correct relationship of limbs to the body.

In the following examples, the stick figures illustrate the notated positions.

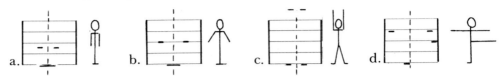

In (a) the hands are written exactly half way between the waist line and the knee line. This represents the lowest position of the hands in relation to the body without another action occurring.

In (b) the level sign representing the feet together is twice as long as the sign for one foot.

In (c) the hands are at their maximum distance above the head without any other action occurring. They are written at the height of one space of the stave above the top line.

In (d) the hands and right foot are shown at their furthest distance from the centre of the frame.

Perform this sequence:

The double line indicates the end of the sequence.

Copy out this sequence and add two more squares:

Front Sign

| A vertical stroke represents a hand or a foot which is *in front* of the body.

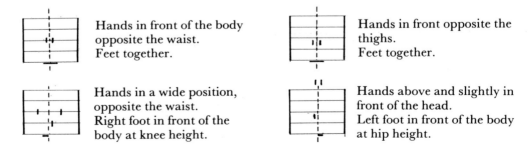

Hands in front of the body opposite the waist. Feet together.

Hands in front opposite the thighs. Feet together.

Hands in a wide position, opposite the waist. Right foot in front of the body at knee height.

Hands above and slightly in front of the head. Left foot in front of the body at hip height.

Write this sequence 'to the other side' i.e. showing the left leg lifting in front, opening to the side and returning.

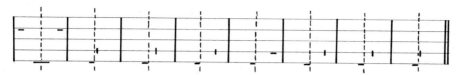

The arms do not move during this sequence. They are therefore shown only at the beginning.

'Behind the Body' Sign

● A dot represents a hand or foot which is *behind* the body.

   Hands behind the body at waist height. Feet apart.

   Hands behind in a wide position just below the top of the head. Feet together.

   Right foot behind the body at knee height. Arms level at shoulder height.

   Left foot behind, just above knee height. Arms level, just above waist height.

Write this sequence 'to the other side'.

Copy out and add the names you use for these positions of the arms:

a.   b.   c.   d.   e.

f.   g.   h.   i.

Write out these positions to the other side:

j.   k.   l.   m.   n.   o.

117

Positions of the Feet

When the feet are in contact with the floor, we need to know whether they are flat, on the ball of the foot or on the tip of the toe.

	Flat Below the Floor Line	Half Point Through the Floor Line	Full Point Above the Floor Line
1st position			
2nd position			
3rd position			
4th position			
5th position			

Third and fifth positions are represented by a qualified feet-together sign. The 'behind' sign is added to the appropriate side to tell you which foot is behind.

In 4th positions, the weight is equally shared by both feet, therefore the front sign and the 'behind' sign must be used.

N.B. These positions may be performed with full turn-out, 45° turn-out or with feet parallel.

118

Foot exercises with simple changes of weight.

Copy out exercise (a).

a.

Write out (b) 'To the other side'.

b.

Bend Signs

Knee bends and Elbow bends are represented by crosses.

Level Bend Sign

The most important part of this cross is the Level sign. It tells you to bend your knee or elbow level with your body.

Think of a small plié.
Note that the bend signs have lowered.

Because the knees are bent level with the body, the feet will be fully turned out. This follows a natural movement rule; the knee should always be in line with the toes.

Examples:

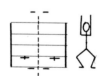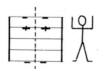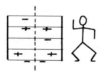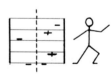

Whenever the knees and elbows are bent, the bend signs must be shown. If no bend signs are shown, the limbs are straight.

Copy out this sequence:

Front Bend Sign

The most important part of this cross is the Front sign. It tells you to bend your knee or elbow in front of the body.

This frame shows a small plié with 45° turn-out. Remember that your knees must be in line with your toes.

This frame shows a small plié with the knees together. The feet are therefore parallel.

Notice the effect of the different bend signs on the direction of the feet:

The feet start fully turned out; they swivel to 45° turn-out; then to a parallel position; they return to 45° turn-out and finish fully turned out.

Write the above sequence with the feet in first position.

Write out the following sequence:

'Behind the body' Bend Sign.

✕   An ordinary cross.

This cross tells you to bend your arm or leg behind the body.

This frame shows the elbows bent behind the body with the hands below them.

Copy out this sequence:

Note the changing relationship of the hands to the elbows.

Write the next sequence 'to the other side'

Note the changing relationship of the foot to the knee.

Compose a sequence which includes these positions:

Contact

/   This is a Right Contact sign. It represents your right hand, or right foot, when it is in contact with another part of you.

\   This is a Left Contact sign. It represents your left hand, or left foot, when it is in contact.

The placing of these signs in the stave tells you which parts are in contact. The dotted line is now omitted.

Compare (a) with (b).

(a)

Right hand in contact with the *right* side of the face.

(b)

Right hand in contact with the *left* side of the face.

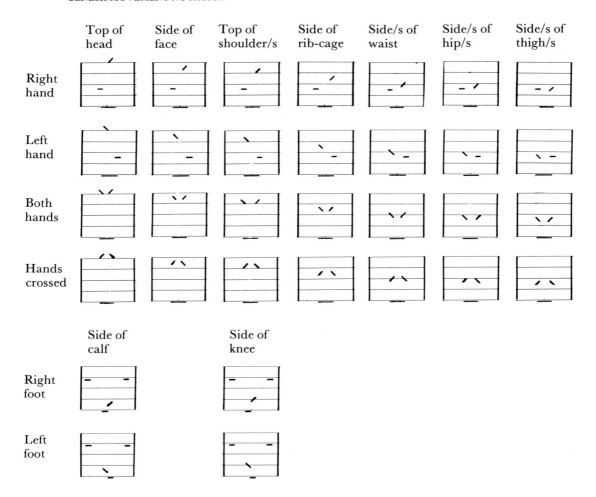

Contacting the Front or Back of the Leg

When a *foot* contacts the front or back of the other leg, the front sign or open dot qualification is placed at the *top* of the contact sign.

The front sign is drawn at right angles to the contact sign to produce a new, distinctive sign. Note that the front sign is shorter than the contact sign.

(a)   right foot in contact with the front of the left shin.
(b)   right foot in contact with the front of the left knee.
(c)   left foot in contact with the back of the right knee.
(d)   left foot in contact with the back of the right calf.

'Automatic Bends'

When you put your hands on your waist you automatically bend your elbows. When your right foot touches your left knee, the right knee has to bend.

When contact signs are used without bend signs, it means that either i) the position of the 'automatic bend' is not important – the knees or elbows may be in any relationship to the feet or hands – or ii) the position of the 'automatic bend' is known from the style or technique of the dance.

Bend signs are used with contact signs i) when their relationship is an exception to the rule, eg. a parallel position in Classical ballet and ii) when you wish to specify the position of the elbows or knees for reasons of emphasis or clarity.

Notate the following positions. Do not record 'automatic bends':

a. *Right hand on your left shoulder*
    Left hand on the right side of your waist
    Feet in 3rd position with the left foot behind.

b. *The above position on the other side.*

c. *Right foot in contact with the back of your left knee*
    Left hand in contact with your left thigh
    Right hand on your left hip.

d. *The above position on the other side.*

Closing Signs

Many dance exercises include the instruction 'Close your foot'.

Closing in First Position

The appropriate contact sign is attached to the feet – together sign.

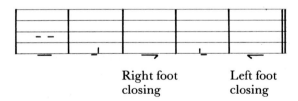

Right foot   Left foot
closing   closing

Closing in Fifth Position

When closing in front, the front sign is used.

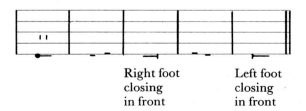

Right foot   Left foot
closing   closing
in front   in front

When closing behind, an *open* dot is used.

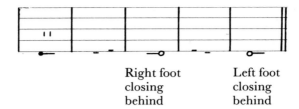

Right foot
closing
behind

Left foot
closing
behind

Closing in Third Position

Right foot
in front

Right foot
behind

Left foot
in front

Left foot
behind

Summary

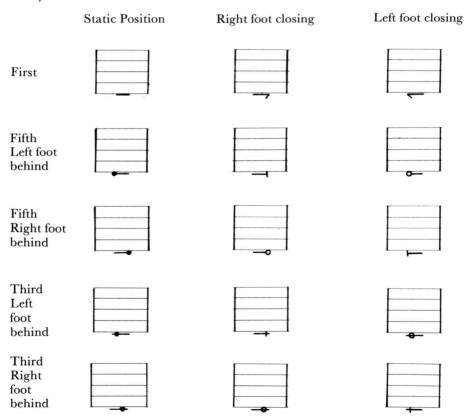

	Static Position	Right foot closing	Left foot closing
First			
Fifth Left foot behind			
Fifth Right foot behind			
Third Left foot behind			
Third Right foot behind			

Each of the next three exercises includes a full plié.

Note that the first, third and fifth positions are written through the floor line to show that the heels are raised at the depth of the plié.

Write exercise (a) 'to the other side' using 5th position and full turn-out:

(a)

Write exercise (b) 'to the other side' using 1st position and 45° turn-out:

(b)

Write exercise (c) 'to the other side' using full turn-out:

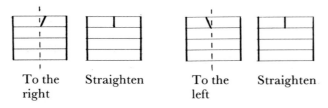

(c)

Head Movements
Use the top space of the stave.

Tilts

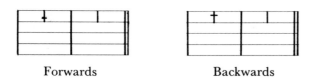

| To the right | Straighten | To the left | Straighten |

A straight line is used to show the head returning to its normal position. It is not necessary to draw this sign if you start with the head straight.

Dotted lines are now included only to clarify the drawing of tilts.

Bends

Forwards   Backwards

Here, the chin has lowered and then lifted.

Turns

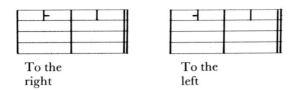

To the right	To the left

When looking from behind the dancer, think of the nose appearing on the right and then on the left.

Upper Body Movements

Use the second space from the top of the stave.

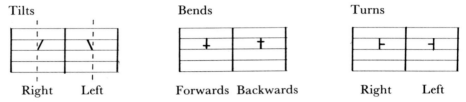

Tilts			Bends		Turns	
Right	Left		Forwards	Backwards	Right	Left

The Head and Body Connection

When you move the upper body, the head goes with that movement.

Tilts

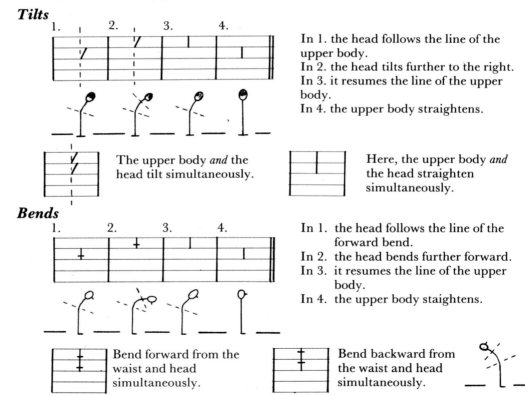

In 1. the head follows the line of the upper body.
In 2. the head tilts further to the right.
In 3. it resumes the line of the upper body.
In 4. the upper body straightens.

The upper body *and* the head tilt simultaneously.

Here, the upper body *and* the head straighten simultaneously.

Bends

In 1. the head follows the line of the forward bend.
In 2. the head bends further forward.
In 3. it resumes the line of the upper body.
In 4. the upper body staightens.

Bend forward from the waist and head simultaneously.

Bend backward from the waist and head simultaneously.

126

Turns

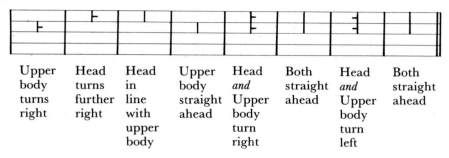

Upper body turns right	Head turns further right	Head in line with upper body	Upper body straight ahead	Head *and* Upper body turn right	Both straight ahead	Head *and* Upper body turn left	Both straight ahead

Counteraction

Tilts

1. Tilt your upper body to the right.
2. Put your head in an upright position.
3. Put your upper body in an upright position. (Your head is tilted to the left.)
4. Straighten your head.

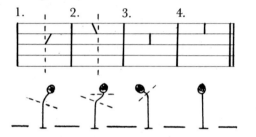

When 1. and 2. are performed simultaneously, the head stays upright.

Bends

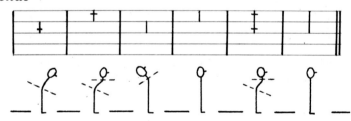

The counteraction in frame 2. results in you looking straight ahead. You have raised your head and therefore you are no longer looking toward the floor.

In frame 5, the simultaneous movements mean that you stay looking straight ahead.

Turns

In frame 2, you look straight ahead.

In frames 5 and 7, you stay looking straight ahead.

The Arm and Body Connection

Arms are notated in relation to the upright body. They are always affected by movement of the body.

Tilts

In sequences (a) and (b), the arms are carried with the movement of the body.

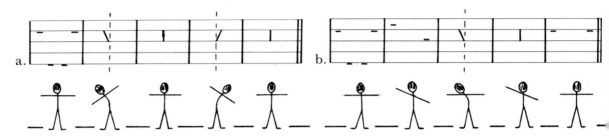

In sequences (c) and (d), the arms move with the body *and* in relation to the body.

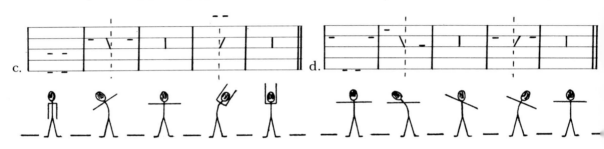

Perform this sequence:

Bends

In frame 4, the hands are plotted opposite the 'upright' waist.
The upper body bend raises the height of the arms.
In frame 6, the hands are opposite the 'upright' shoulders.
The body bend lowers the arms.

Turns

In frames 4 and 6, new relationships of the arms to the body are shown.

Lower Body Movement:

Body movements which occur in the hip joints are written in the third space from the top of the stave.

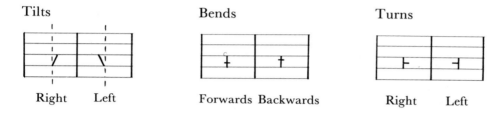

Tilts		Bends		Turns	
Right	Left	Forwards	Backwards	Right	Left

Counteractions

Tilts

Write out the next two sequences to 'the other side'.

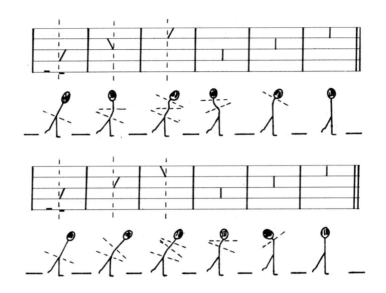

Bends

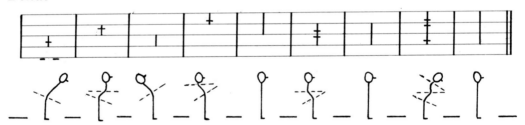

Turns

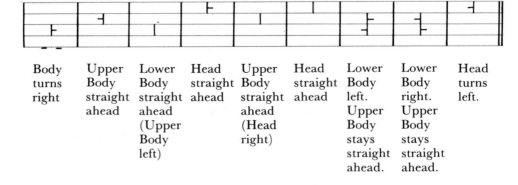

Body turns right	Upper Body straight ahead	Lower Body straight ahead (Upper Body left)	Head straight ahead	Upper Body straight ahead (Head right)	Head straight ahead	Lower Body left. Upper Body stays straight ahead.	Lower Body right. Upper Body stays straight ahead.	Head turns left.

The Leg and Body Connection

Legs are notated in relation to the upright body.

Tilts

In frames 2 and 3, the body tilts and then returns to normal, the arms and legs maintaining the same relationship to the body.

Frames 4 and 5 illustrate the difference between the Leg and Body Connection and the Arm and Body Connection.

In frame 4, the sign representing the foot is shown again at hip height. It is therefore *not* carried with the body movement.

In frame 5, the sign representing the foot is again re-stated. The foot stays at hip height. If the sign representing the foot had not been shown in frame 5, the foot would have been carried with the body movement e.g.

Perform this sequence:

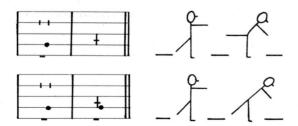

Bends

Lower body bends work in the same way as lower body tilts.

Both the arms and the legs have moved with the body.

The right foot has stayed at knee height.

131

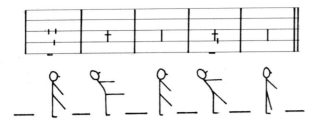

In frame 2., both the arms and legs have moved with the body.
In frame 4., the right foot has stayed at knee height.
In frame 5., the right leg has lowered keeping its relationship to the body as shown in 4.

Write this sequence to the other side.

Turns

A turn of the hips will always affect the position of a leg in space (as well as the whole spine, head and arms).

   Here you are, in effect, facing the Right Front Corner. It is only your left leg which has not moved.

Describe where your left foot is 'pointing' in frames 4, 6 and 8:

Assume a turn of 45°.
e.g. Frame 2. The left foot is pointing towards the Right Back Corner.

Combining Two Head Movements

Tilt and Bend

To the right and forwards

To the left and backwards

Tilt and Turn

Tilt left and turn left

Tilt right and turn left

Bend and Turn

Forwards and to the right

N.B.

Both equations give the same results.

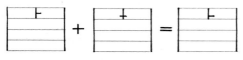

Remember to bend forwards toward your chest. Only the turn is to the left.

Backward and to the left

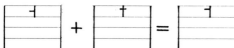

Again, the same resultant positions.

Experiment with combinations of all three movements – tilts, bends and turns

e.g.

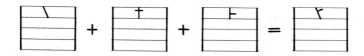

Combining Two Upper Body Movements

Experiment in the same way as described for combining two head movements. Remember to take your head and arms with you!

The arms stay level with the shoulders. The body tilt creates a diagonal design of the arms.

Here the body movement creates a parallel design of the arms.

Combining Two Lower Body Movements

The turn makes the right foot point to the right.
The bend backwards raises the height of the right leg.
The arms have moved with the body.

Again, the turn makes the right foot point to the right.
By restating the foot, it has stayed at knee height.

Sequences of Combinations of Body Movements

Always read body movements from the bottom of the stave upwards.

Compare Sequence a. with b.

a.

In frame 3, the head bends forwards in new direction faced by the upper body.

Frames 1, 2 and 3 performed simultaneously.

b.

In frame 3, the upper body bends forwards toward the new direction faced by the hips.

Frames 1, 2 and 3 performed simultaneously.

Examples of limbering

a.

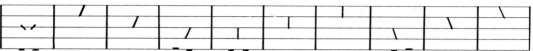

b.

c.

Make up your own exercises using counteractions and combinations of tilts, bends and turns.

'Contractions'

Keeping your shoulders over your hips
push the middle of your back backwards.

Your spine will now be in a rounded shape – a concave curve.

This movement is commonly called a contraction. There are many different kinds of contractions. Here, we will use:

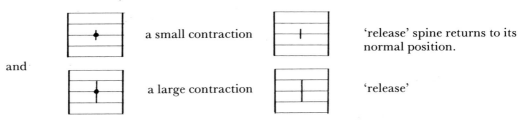

a small contraction

'release' spine returns to its normal position.

and

a large contraction

'release'

Perform this sequence:

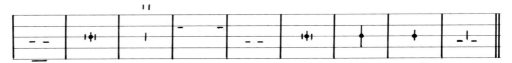

Head Displacements

Returns
to
normal

Right   Left   Forwards   Backwards

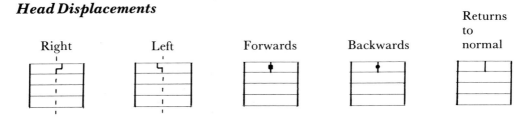

Upper Body Displacements

Returns
to
normal

Right   Left   Forwards   Backwards

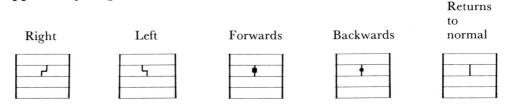

N.B. This movement is sometimes called a contraction of the upper body.

Shoulder Movements

Right Shoulder

| Forward | Raised | Backwards | Dropped | Return to Normal |

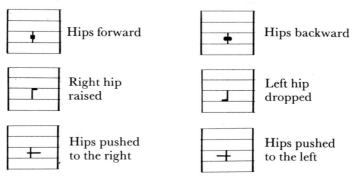

Write these positions for the left shoulder.

Hip Movements

Hips forward

Hips backward

Right hip raised

Left hip dropped

Hips pushed to the right

Hips pushed to the left

Write 'to the other side':

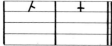

Frames 1.–3. show a circle of the right hip.
4.–6. show a circle of the left shoulder.
7.–11. show a head roll to the left.

Make up a sequence of isolated head and body movements.

Kneeling

A curved contact sign shows a part of the body in contact with the floor.

⌐ This right curve relates to the right side of the body.

⌐ This left curve relates to the left side of the body.

Kneeling

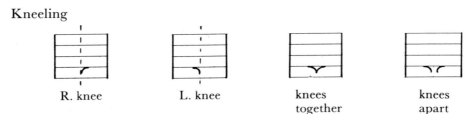

| R. knee | L. knee | knees together | knees apart |

Note that the signs hang from the knee line.

Write this sequence to the other side:

In the final frame, the front knee is shown bent at knee height, its distance from the floor.

Perform these sequences:

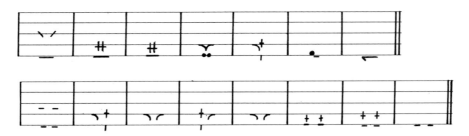

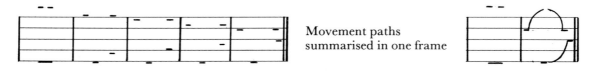

Movement Lines

Movement lines trace the paths of limbs, acting as a visual aid and summarising a series of intermediary positions.

Paths Level with the Body

I. Performed with straight limbs.

The extremity (hand or foot), and therefore the movement line, traces an outward arc.

Movement paths summarised in one frame

Attach movement lines to the *final* position.

Draw movement lines finely. They should be thinner than the signs they join.

II. Performed by bending limbs.

The extremity, and therefore the movement line, traces an inward arc.

138

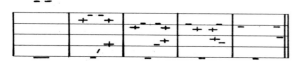 

Paths in Front of or Behind the Body

As we notate as if we are behind the dancer movement paths directly in front of or behind the body trace straight lines.

To show when a straight path is traced by a straight limb, a slight outward arc is drawn.

To show when a straight path is traced by a bending limb, a slight inward arc is drawn.

Outward Arcs

 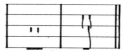

Inward Arcs

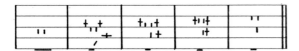 

Copy out the following sequence:

Write the next two sequences 'to the other side'.

No movement line is required when the leg lowers without bending.

Qualified Movement Lines
Paths in Front of the Body

Draw this movement path in one frame

Beware! This frame shows an inward curve of the arms. More information is required to take the arms in front of the body.

Front signs are added to the movement lines, being drawn at right angles to the lines.

Copy out 1(a) and 1(b).

1a.

1b.

Write 2(a) and 2(b) 'to the other side'.

2a.

2b.

Write 3(a) and 3(b) 'to the other side'.

3a.

3b.

Write 4(a) and 4(b) 'to the other side'.

4a.

4b.

Paths Behind the Body

Draw this movement path in one frame

Remember: The arms will bend to trace an inward curve. More information is required to take the arms behind the body.

'Behind' signs are added to the movement lines.

Copy out sequences 1(a) and 1(b).

1a.

1b.

Write 2(a) and 2(b) 'to the other side'.

2a.    2b.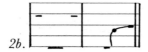

Write 3(a) and 3(b) 'to the other side'.

3a.    3b.

Write 4(a) and 4(b) 'to the other side'.

4a. 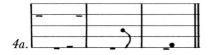   4b.

Paths in Front of and Behind the Body

By combining the theory already described, these movements are readily summarised.

Copy out the next three sequences 'to the other side'.

a.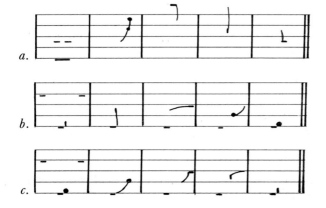

b.

c.

Paths Directly in Front of and Behind the Body

Swinging movement of arms

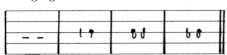

Swinging movement of the leg

The outward arc of the movement line is attached to the final position to denote that the whole movement has been performed with an extended limb.

Horizontal Paths

Movement Lines describing limbs that move *parallel to the ground* are drawn with a very slight upward curve for movement in front of the body, and a very slight downward curve for movement behind the body.

Examples:

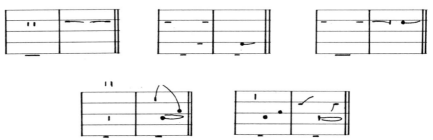

Changes in height are drawn as they are seen from behind the dancer.

Examples:

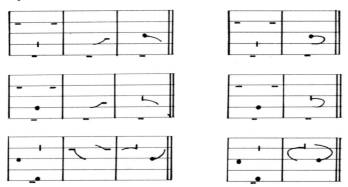

Describe the following 'pairs' of movements:

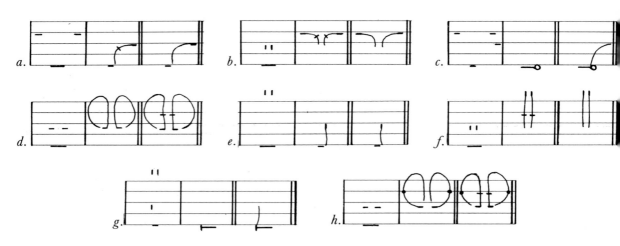

SUMMARY – IN-STAVE INFORMATION

Part II has dealt with:
1. positions of the arms and legs
2. head and body movements
3. simple changes of weight
4. simple changes of level, and
5. spatial paths of the arms and legs.

Choose a movement idea such as circles. Think of circular movements for different parts of your body.

e.g.

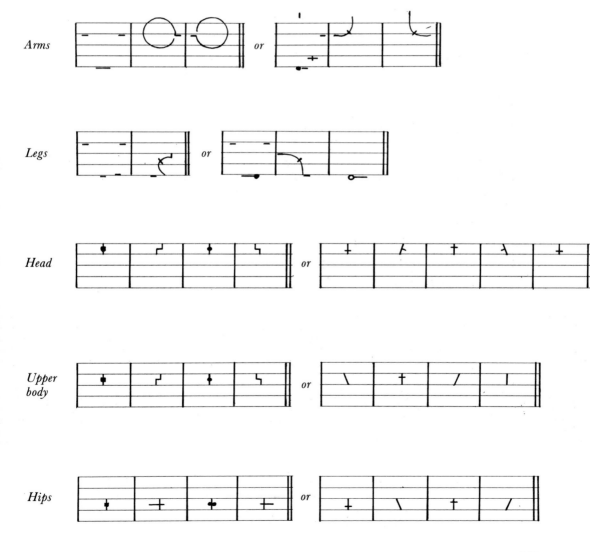

Explore combinations of spatial paths.

e.g.

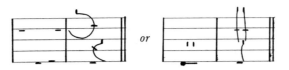 *or*

Combine contrary body movements e.g. a clockwise movement and an anti-clockwise movement.

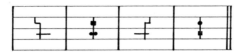

Explore 'reversing' movements.

Compare (a) with (b)

In both sequences, the weight is transferred forwards and then backwards.

In sequence (a) the arms move in front of the body, over the head and then behind the body.

In sequence (b) the spatial paths of the arms are reversed.

Experiment with changes of level.

e.g.

 *or*

Compose a dance study based on your choice of movement idea.

Reminder – consider movements which are isolated, simultaneous, contrasting, 'opposed' and 'reversed'.

Part III
Above-stave information

Pulse Beat

ϕ This sign represents the pulse or main beat of a dance rhythm.

Think of working in phrases of four regular beats.

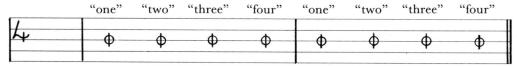

In Part III, the pulse beat is written in the stave to represent movement.

The number which tells you the length of each phrase is written in the top two spaces of the stave.

A space is left for your starting position. This space has no time value.

A vertical line is drawn after your starting position to show the beginning of the phrase. The next vertical line shows the end of one phrase and the beginning of the next.

The double line shows the end of the sequence.

You may wish to use irregular phrases.

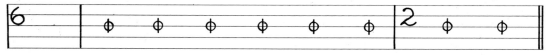

A phrase of six beats, followed by a phrase of two beats.

Note that there is no space after the number two because the phrase of two beats immediately follows the phrase of six.

Holding a Position
If no movement occurs on a beat i.e. you are holding a position, the 'missing' beat is shown above the stave.

Clap the rhythm shown by the pulse beats in the stave:

The "missing" beats i.e. the held positions, occur on beats "three" and "five".

Half-beats

This sign represents a half beat. It is called 'an'.

When a pulse beat is followed by a half-beat, the value of the pulse beat is halved.

Clap these rhythms:

Quarter-beats

This sign represents the quarter-beat between ⏀ and ⏀. It is called 'té'.

This sign represents the quarter-beat between ⏀ and ⏀. It is called 'ti'.

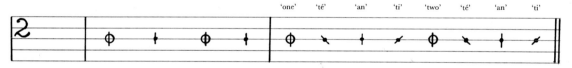

When a pulse beat is followed by ↘ 'té', the value of the pulse beat is a quarter of the whole beat.

When a pulse beat is followed by ↗ 'ti', the value of the pulse beat is three-quarters of the whole beat.

Clap these rhythms:

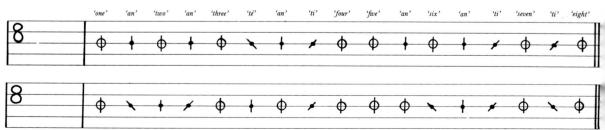

Third-beats

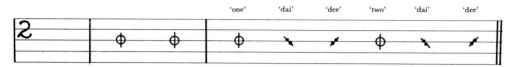 This sign represents the third-beat after Φ. It is called 'dai'.

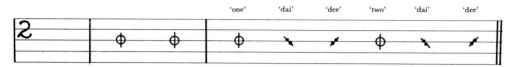 This sign represents the third-beat before Φ. It is called 'dee'.

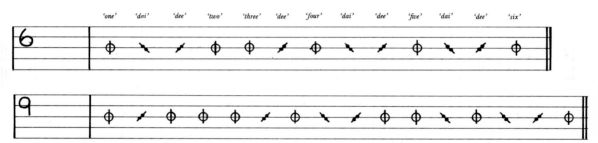

When a pulse beat is followed by ↘ 'dai', the value of the pulse beat is a third of the whole beat.

When a pulse beat is followed by ↗ 'dee', the value of the pulse beat is two-thirds of the whole beat.

Clap these rhythms:

Tempo

You may wish to show the tempo (speed) of your dance by the use of one of the following instructions:

Fast, Moderately Fast, Moderate, Moderately Slow, As Slow as Possible or As Fast as Possible.

The tempo can be made more specific e.g. 60 beats per minute, by giving the pulse beat a metronomic speed i.e. Φ = 60.

Instructions as shown in music scores may also be used e.g.

Adagio – very slow and leisurely
Andante – a leisurely walking pace
Allegretto – lively
Allegro – lively but quicker than Allegretto

Clap the following rhythms:

Fast

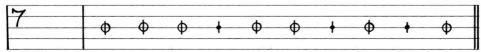

Andante

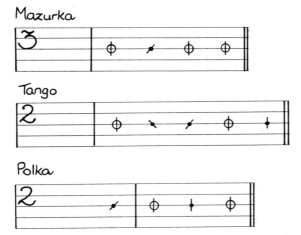

Common Dance Rhythms

Mazurka

Tango

Polka

These examples illustrate a typical rhythm of one bar of each of the dances.

Music is commonly notated in bars – regular divisions of time. You can use the same divisions for your dance, the vertical lines becoming bar lines and the number referring to the time signature i.e. the number of main beats per bar.

Write bar lines immediately before beat one.

Polka

When the *last* beat of a bar is 'missing' – not used, it is not necessary to write it in. See bar 4 above.

Jig

The use of third-beats shows that the main beat is divisible by three. The first bar above shows a rhythm commonly used for jumping. Skipping naturally follows this rhythm. Hop on ✗ 'dee'. Step on ⏀ the main beat. You are in the air on ⟍ 'dai'.

Legato Line

A Legato Line is used to show continuous movement. It is a curved line written above the stave.

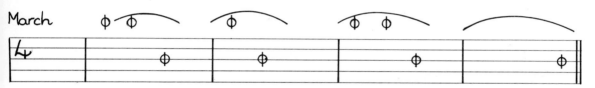

Move on beat "one". Hold beat "two".
Move on beats "three" and "four".
The Legato line is written over beats "five", "six" and "seven".
Move on beat "eight".

The Legato line links the 'missing' beats – "five" and "six" – with the pulse beat which represents movement on beat "seven".

The Legato line tells you to start moving on beat "five", continue moving through beat "six" and complete the movement on beat "seven".

The movement is written on beat 'seven' because that is when the movement is completed.

Bar 1. – Hold beat "one". Start moving on beat "two" and stop on beat "three". Hold on beat "four".

Bar 2. – Start moving on beat "one" and stop on beat "two". Hold beats "three" and "four".

Bar 3. – Start moving on beat "one", continue through beat "two" and stop on beat "three". Hold beat "four".

Bar 4. – Start moving on beat "one", continue through beats "two" and "three" and stop on beat "four". The 'missing' beats are not shown because the length of the bar is shown.

Dance Phrase Line

You may wish to compose a dance which has no direct relationship to its aural accompaniment.

You may wish to dance in silence.

In these studies, use Dance Phrase lines to identify phrases.

A Dance Phrase line is a broken line curved to join the stave, spanning the relevant length.

This shows the idea of the Dance Phrase line

Here three phrases are shown.

Canon

The Canon sign identifies the phrase or sequence which is to be performed at a different time by another dancer or dancers.

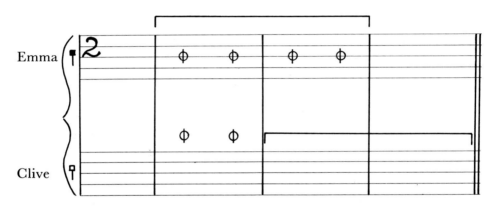

Emma ⊤ performs a sequence of four beats

Clive ⊤ performs the same sequence, starting one bar later.

Stave Linking
Staves are linked by the bar lines or phrase lines.

The bracket ⎰⎱ shows that the movements of the dancers are related.

The number of beats per bar is shown only in the top stave.

Stave Labelling
Use identification signs e.g. Emma ⊤ and Clive ⊤ to label the staves.

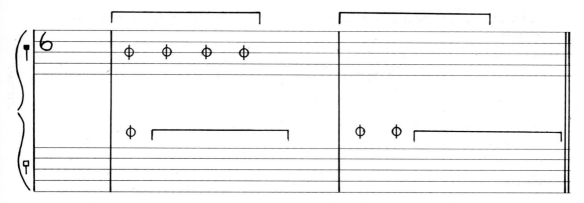

Emma performs a sequence
of 4 beats. Clive performs
the same sequence, starting
one beat later. Emma
repeats the sequence after
waiting two beats. Clive
waits for three beats.

SUMMARY – ABOVE-STAVE INFORMATION

We can now look at Rhythm and Phrases in some detail.

We have used three systems – 1. Counts, 2. Bar Lines and 3. Dance Phrases.

Compose a sequence using this tempo and rhythm:

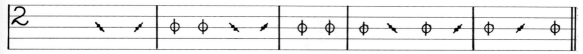

Compose a sequence using this tempo and rhythm:

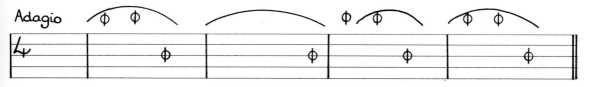

Write out the rhythm of a dance study which you have learnt. Use counts or bar lines.

Compose a four bar dance study using one of the following dance rhythms:

Mazurka, Tango or Polka.

Write out the rhythm of your study.

Part IV
Linking information

In Part IV, vertical lines are no longer used to define a frame.
They will show the beginning and end of a bar, sequence or phrase as described in Part III.

Jumping
A jump is shown by a curved line below the stave.

On the spot

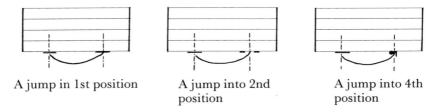

A jump in 1st position   A jump into 2nd position   A jump into 4th position

The dotted lines are drawn here as a guide to show the start and finish of the jump line.

These jumps are from two feet to two feet.

More 'automatic bends'
Because it is usual to bend your knees in preparation for a jump and on landing from a jump, there is no need to record these knee bends. Pliés for jumps are notated only when they are choreographically important e.g. when a landing plié is held.

Forwards
The front sign is added to the jump line.

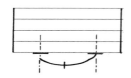

A jump forwards in 1st

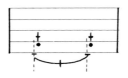

A hop forwards on the left foot

Backwards

A 'behind the body' sign is added to the jump line.

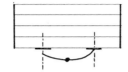

A jump backwards in 1st

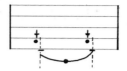

A hop backwards on the right foot

Sideways

To show a jump to the right, the jump line joins the *nearest* side of the notated landing position.

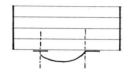

A jump in 1st to the right

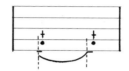

A hop to the right on the left foot

To show a jump to the left, the jump line joins the *furthest* side of the notated landing position.

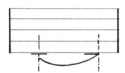

A jump in 1st to the left

A hop to the left on the right foot

Summary

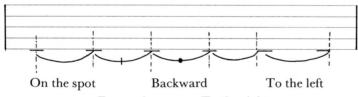

On the spot   Backward   To the left

Forward   To the right

Rhythm of Jumps

The duration of jumps is dictated by the rhythm of landing.

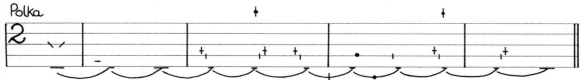

Write out the previous sequence using the following rhythm:

Aerial Position

You may wish to change position in the air.

The legs stretch in 4th position between the 3rd and 4th jumps.

Note that, in this example, the time value of the aerial position is dictated by the rhythm of the landing of the preceding and following jumps.

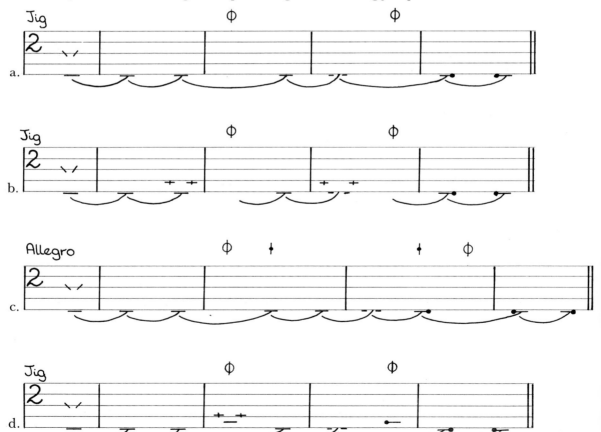

In (a) bars 2 and 3 show jumps taking two whole beats.
Because the jump line starts before the 'missing' beat and finishes on the next beat, you are in the air on the 'missing' beats – beat "one" of bar 2 and beat "two" of bar 3.

In (b) the 'missing' beats are held, the jump line starting underneath but including the 'missing' beat.

In (c) you are again in the air on the 'missing' beat. In bar 2 you land on a sub-beat. In bar 3 you take off on a sub-beat.

Compare (a) with (b)

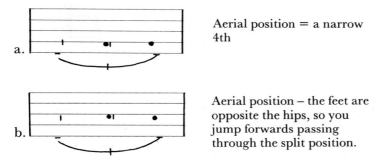

a. Aerial position = a narrow 4th

b. Aerial position – the feet are opposite the hips, so you jump forwards passing through the split position.

Compose a sequence of jumps. Include a jump lasting two beats, a varying rhythm and an aerial position.

Running

Running is a series of jumps from one foot to the other.

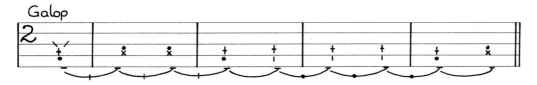

Galop

Bar 1. shows two runs forward.
Bar 2. shows two hops.
Bar 3. shows two runs backward.
Bar 4. shows two hops.

When notating running, it is not always necessary to show the raised leg.

The above sequence starts with two runs, the first run onto the right foot, the second onto the left foot.

Free Runs

You may wish to notate running without specifying the timing or number of runs.

Write two runs close together add ditto marks --- and a travelling sign to show the path of travel.

Runs forward

Runs backward

Extract – "Dances of Love and Death" – Cohan/Britten

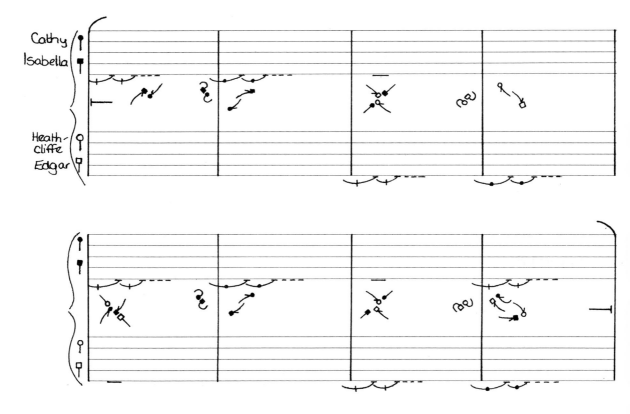

Stepping

A step line traces the path of your step.

On the spot

With the right foot

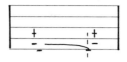

With the left foot

Forwards

A step with the right foot; the left foot is behind at knee height

A step with the left foot; the right foot contacting the left knee

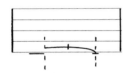

A low step with the right foot

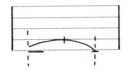

A high step with the left foot

As in running, it is not always necessary to show the raised leg.

Backwards

A low step with the left foot; the right foot is in front at knee height.

A high step with the right foot; left foot hip height

Into 4th Position

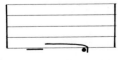 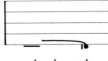  

Right foot forwards   backwards   Left foot forwards   backwards

Because the step line joins the front, or 'behind' sign, thus giving the direction of the step, there is no need to qualify the step line, i.e. add information to the step line.

Extract – "The Rite of Spring" – MacMillan/Stravinsky

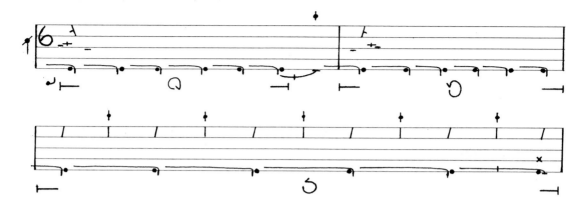

Sideways

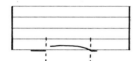

A low step to the right, with the right foot.

A high step to the left, with the left foot.

Summary

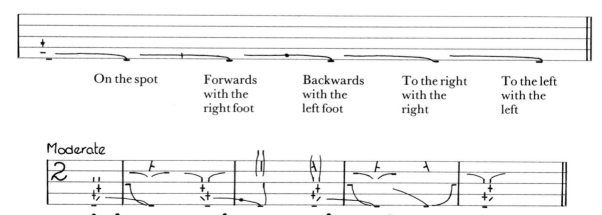

On the spot	Forwards with the right foot	Backwards with the left foot	To the right with the right	To the left with the left

Moderate

Note that the changes of direction occur *before* the steps.

Free walks

A quick way of notating'walk freely' is to use a short version of the series of 4th's.

Walk forwards

Note that the first walk is with the right foot. The first 4th position is therefore •ı

Walk backwards

The first 4th position notated ı• shows the right foot behind.

Design a floor pattern.

e.g.

Use a series of low, high or combined steps to travel between selected locations.

e.g.

Combining Jumps and Steps.

Waltz

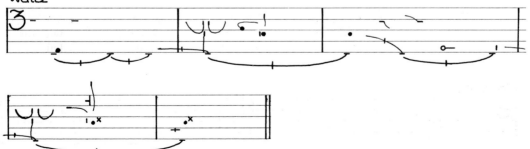

Note the use of two kinds of preparation for big jumps i) 'run, run, step' and ii) a galop preparation.

Extract – "Four Schumann Pieces" – Van Manen/Schumann

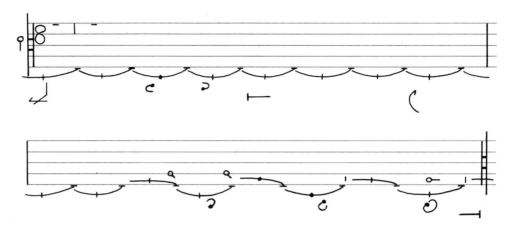

Extract – "Voluntaries" – Tetley/Poulenc

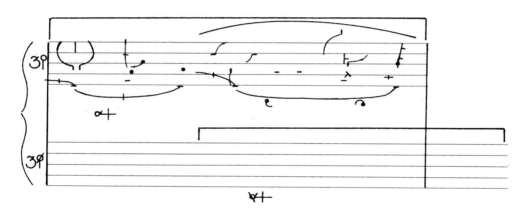

Sliding the Feet

A slide line is a straight line written below the stave.

Forwards

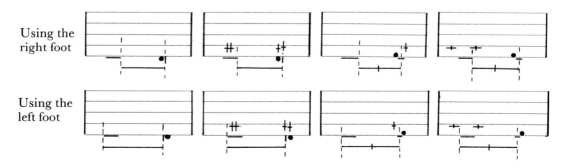

Using the right foot

Using the left foot

Backwards

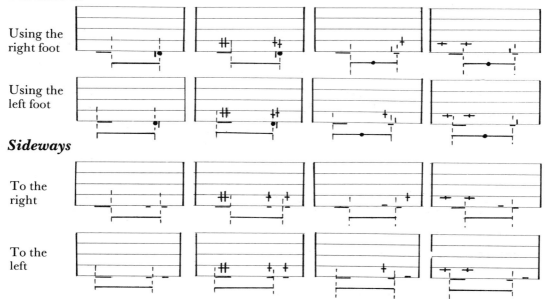

Using the right foot

Using the left foot

Sideways

To the right

To the left

Into 4th Positions

Note how the size of the fourth is dictated by the relationship of the knees to the body.

Summary

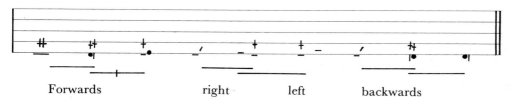

| Forwards | right | left | backwards |

Extract – "The Rite of Spring" – Alston/Stravinsky

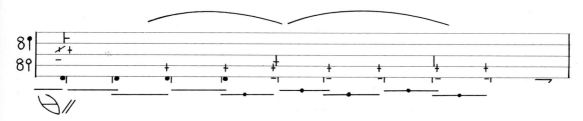

Extract – 1st Song of "Ghost Dances" – Bruce/South American Folk Songs.

Compose a sequence which includes jumping, stepping and sliding.

Repeated Patterns of Movement

Repeat Signs
Repeat Signs are sets of parallel lines which enclose the movements to be repeated.

Repeat *the same way*

Example A

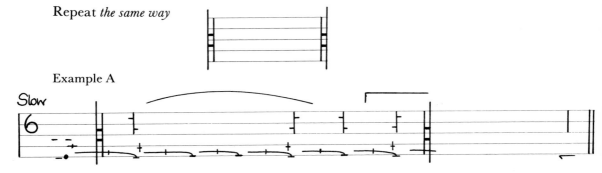

Exclusion Sign
Information below the exclusion sign ⌐‾‾‾ is not performed at the end of the repeat. In example A, a new ending is shown.

Leave an 'empty' space for the repeat. The length of the space is non-specific. If you are using bars, the number of 'empty' bars is indicated. See example B.

Example B.

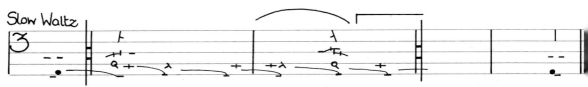

Repeat to the *other* side

162

Example C.

'Fin'

The word 'Fin' indicates the final position of the repeat. Information following this instruction is performed only at the start of the repeat.

Example D.

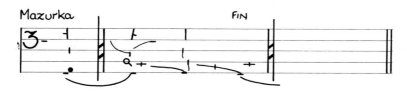

Repeat on *alternate* sides

Example E.

The number of repeats is written in the middle two spaces of the stave. This sequence is performed *four* times in all, in varying directions.

Read the following extract from Act IV 'La Bayadère' – Petipa/Minkus.

Note the number of repeats.
The dancer who leads the entrance of The Shades has to perform a high arabesque on the same leg 38 times!

Irregular Repeats

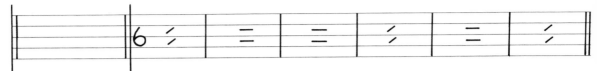

The first repeat is a reflection of the enclosed movement i.e. 'to the other side'. The second repeat is the same as the enclosed movement, and so on.

These repeat instructions are also used to show movement performed by different dancers in varying ways.

The in-stave repeat instruction refers to the movement notated in the top stave.

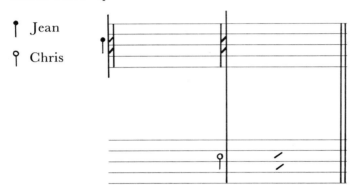

Chris 'reflects' Jean. In this example, he dances the movement as notated in the first bar of Jean's stave.

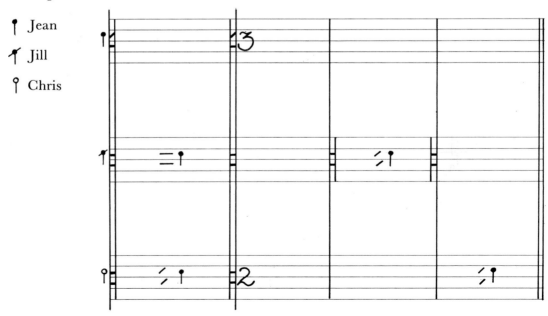

Jill first performs in the same way as Jean, Chris first 'reflects' Jean.
On the first repeat – Jill reflects Jean, Chris is the same as Jean.
On the second repeat – Jill and Chris both reflect Jean.
On the last repeat – Jill is the same as Jean, Chris reflects Jean.

CONCLUSION

The tasks which follow illustrate two ways of using components from *each* Part of this section of the book.

Task 1.

a.　　*Devise a motif.*

e.g.

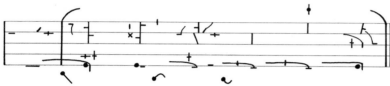

b.　　*Add the use of repetition and direction.*

c.　　*Vary the repetition and directions.*

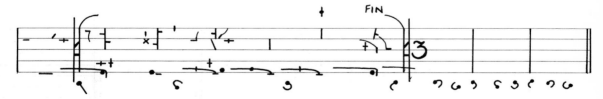

d.　　*Change levels and vary the body movements.*

e.   *Vary the rhythm and phrasing.*

f.   *Vary the Tempo and floor pattern.*

N.B. You do not have to follow this order of development and variation.

Task 2.

a.   *Choose three positions which can be performed in sequence.*

e.g.

Position 1	Position 2	Position 3

b.   *Perform these positions in sequence.*

Slow

c.   *Add a variation of this sequence to create a phrase of 6.*

d.   *Change the rhythm and add legato lines.*

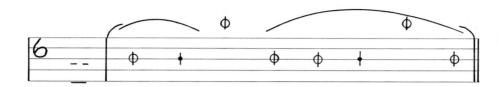

e.   *Teach version (d) to several dancers. Experiment with the dancers performing the sequence, perhaps at the same time but in different directions.*

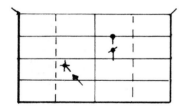

f.   *Observe the effect of the dancers performing the sequence in the same direction but in canon.*

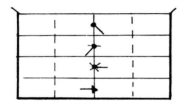

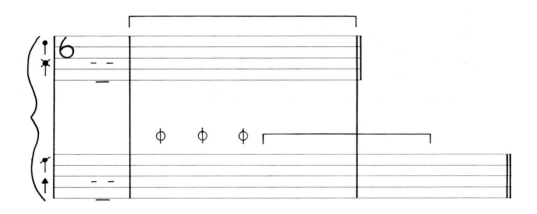

g.   *Vary the number of dancers, directions, and timing of the canon.*

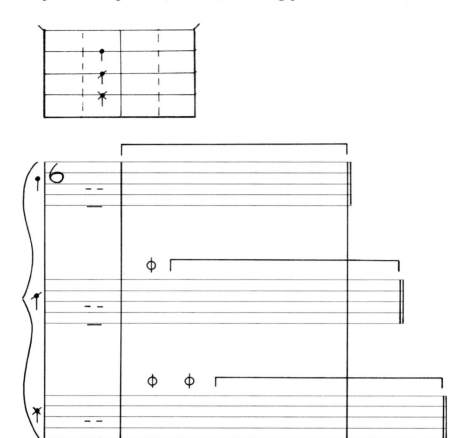

Indexes

Index to
Labanotation

Index to
Benesh Movement Notation